Who Fears to Speak ...?

The Story of Belfast and the 1916 Rising

Gerry Adams

First published 1991
by
Clóbhuailte ag AP/RN Print
58 Cearnóg Pharnell
Baile Atha Cliath

This revised edition published 2001
by
Beyond the Pale Publications
Unit 2.1.2 Conway Mill
5-7 Conway Street
Belfast BT13 2DE

Tel: +44 (0)28 90 438630
Fax: +44 (0)28 90 439707
E-mail: info@btpale.ie
Website: http://www.btpale.ie

All proceeds from the sale of this book go to
Siopa na hEolaine, Bothar na bhFal, Beal Feirste.

British Library Cataloguing-in-Publication Data.
A catalogue record for this book is available from the British Library.

Printed in Dublin by Colour Books Ltd.

To the women of 1916 and today.

Amhrán na bhFiann

Seo dhaoibh, a chairde, duan óglaigh,
Caithréimeach, bríomhar, ceolmhar,
Ar dtinte cnámh go buacach táid,
'S an spéir go mín réaltógach.
Is fonnmhar faobhrach sinn chun gleo,
'S go tiúnmhar glé roimh thíocht don ló,
Faoi chiúnas caomh na hoíche ar seol,
Seo libh, canaig' Amhrán na bhFiann.

Sinne laochra Fáil,
Atá faoi gheall ag Éirinn,
Buíon dár slua
Thar toinn do ráinig chugainn,
Faoi mhóid bheith soar,
Seantír ár sinsear feasta
Ní fhágfar faoin tíorán ná faoin tráill.
Anocht a théim sa bhearna baoil,
Le gean ar Ghaeil chun báis nó saoil,
Le gunna-scréach, faoi lámhach na bpiléar,
Seo libh, canaig' Amhrán na bhFiann.

Cois bánta reidhe, ar arda sléibhe
Ba bhuach ár sinsear romhainn,
Ag lámhach go tréan fá'n sár-bhrat sein,
Atá thuas sa ghaoith go seolta;
Ba dhúchas riamh d'ár gcine cháidh
Gan iompáil siar ó imirt air,
'Siul mar iad I gcoinne namhaid
Seo libh, canaig Amhrán na bhFiann.

A bhuíon nach fann d'fhuil Gaeil is Gall,
Sinn breacadh lae na saoirs,
Tá scéimhle 's scanradh i gcroíthe namhad,
Roimh ranganna laochra ár dtíre;
Ar dtínte is tréith gan spréach anois,
Sin luisne ghlé san spéir anoir,
'S an bíobha i raon na pbiléar agaibh;
Seo libh, canaig Amhrán na bhFiann.

Contents

Introduction to 2001 Edition

Publication of this essay in 1991 was on the anniversary date of the execution of James Connolly and Seán MacDiarmada. It was a little commemorative gesture to mark the 75th anniversary of the Easter Rising.

It is being republished now over ten years later, on the 20th anniversary of the Long Kesh hunger strikes, as my little contribution to and thanks for the work of the Green Cross book shop in Belfast.

'Belfast was the first home of republicanism in Ireland', Terence MacSwiney correctly remarks in the preface of his *Principles of Freedom.* Yet in 1916, during the Easter Rising, Belfast was quiet. Why?

As I said in the earlier edition, this essay tries to answer that question. It spells out the political and social conditions in Belfast from 1900 to 1916 and traces the growth of republicanism in that period. It also sketches the roles of some figures who were later to play a central part in national leadership of the insurrectionists.

The growth of militant unionism, the role of 'constitutional nationalism' and the attitude and omnipresent influence of the British establishment in all of this is also outlined.

Such a study deserves and requires a more substantial manuscript than this one. This slim volume, I am sorry to say, can only scrape the surface of a fascinating period in the history of Belfast city during a traumatic phase of our national history.

In the time between 1991 and now I am also sorry to say that I have not been able to substantially improve or enlarge the original essay. Apart from the appendix – for which I am grateful to John Quinn and UCD Archives Department – and some minor editing, the text is as it was.

However in the same period Belfast city itself has changed utterly. The first home of Irish republicanism is now the most republican city on this island. And because it is so, Belfast is now becoming a shared city with a future for all its people. Belfast will never be the same again.

James Connolly and Seán MacDiarmada, who lived, worked and agitated here, would relish the challenges and opportunities presented and created by the rise of Sinn Féin and the emergence of the party as the largest one in their adopted city. Of course there is a lot yet to be done, nationally as well as locally, before we get to make our own history.

So the sum total of these pages present but a snapshot – a photograph – of a period from our past. The republican history of our city is evolving yet and must wait for another day and another author to tell the full story.

In the meantime my thanks to Pauline, to Siobhan, Tina, Sean and Aengus who helped with the 1991 edition. And to the late Mary Hughes – go ndeanfaidh Dia trocaire uirthi. Thanks also to Marguerite and R.G. for their help with this one. And as always, thanks to Colette.

Beir Bua
Gerry Adams

Belfast
24th June, 2001

1. How does she stand?

'I met with Napper Tandy and he took me by the hand.
He said, 'How is old Ireland and how does she stand?'

('The Wearing of the Green')

In 1870 Isaac Butt was the leader of the Irish Home Rule Party in the British House of Commons. He was one of a long line of Irish parliamentary leaders, including Daniel O'Connell, whose methods were constitutional and whose aim for Ireland was a measure of self-government under the British crown. This measure – Home Rule, as it was called – had little competition in Ireland from the republicans since the failure of the Fenian Rising of 1867. The Home Rule Party was treated with contempt at Westminster. It was able to filibuster and harass its opponents, but its best efforts failed to win the Irish people any relief. Twenty-eight Bills, introduced between 1870 and 1880 and aimed at doing this, were rejected.

These were years of bad harvests in Ireland; starvation was threatening again and the peasants had little confidence in constitutional agitation for reform. Except in Belfast and its hinterlands, where special protective measures applied, the English rulers insisted upon enforcing the principle of free trade in land, with evictions, high rents and taxes. The 'prosperity' of the region around Belfast was primarily the product of its English-sponsored shipbuilding and repairing industry.

Elsewhere, rural Ireland was forced to restrict itself to agriculture, for whose products no market but that of England was available. In the English markets, Irish products had to sell at prices fixed by world competition, while Irish agriculture in general could not advance because it was crippled by parasitic landlordism.

Resistance in rural Ireland grew. It was a Fenian, Michael Davitt, on ticket of leave from prison, who organised the small holders in defence of their homes. The people responded magnificently and with great solidarity. Evictions were resisted and evicted tenants were rehoused and helped. The Land League grew out of this defiance. Rank and file IRB members, or Fenians, were heavily involved. An organisation of Irish women, the Ladies' Land League, supported this resistance.

By 1880, Charles Stewart Parnell was at the head of the Home Rule Party in Westminster. Davitt persuaded him to become the President of the Land League and thus began an alliance of constitutional and other forces.

Parnell's parliamentary policy was clear-cut. He aimed to hold the balance of power between the Conservatives and the Liberals. This campaign was reinforced by the activities of the Land League and the Fenians' organisation with its implicit threat of physical force. The British government could no longer ignore Irish nationalism and its demands.

They dealt with it in traditional fashion. The Land League was proscribed, habeas corpus suspended, meetings baton-charged, and over one thousand were imprisoned, including Davitt and Parnell. To balance this stick, the carrot of a Land Act was introduced and in 1882, Gladstone and Parnell concluded an agreement to pacify, if not settle, the land question. It failed to do either.

At the general elections in 1885 the Home Rule Party, led by Parnell, held the balance of power in the House of Commons.

Ireland was ruled by Coercion Acts, the Land League continued to harass landlords, Parnell and his party harassed Westminster and the Fenians were still perceived to be a threat whose potential was underlined by the actions of the Invincibles. The first Home Rule Bill was introduced by Gladstone in 1886 in an attempt to settle the unrest and agitation.

There was intense Conservative and considerable Liberal opposition to this measure. An alliance of Liberals and Conservatives was formed to protect the Union. It found its vanguard in the Orange Order and was quick to exploit its hostility to Home Rule.

The first Home Rule Bill was defeated and the parliament was dissolved. The Home Rule Party was returned with eighty-six MPs in the subsequent election. There were seventeen anti-Home Rulers and the Conservatives were back in power with Lord Salisbury as Prime Minister.

Coercion continued, the agrarian struggle intensified and the Home Rule campaign went on unabated. As things came to one of their periodic climaxes, a longstanding effort by the British to smear Parnell succeeded in 1890 when he was named as a co-respondent in a celebrated divorce case. He was savaged by the Irish Catholic bishops, his party split and he died the following year, aged forty-five.

In 1893 Gladstone's second Home Rule Bill passed the House of Commons, but was rejected by the House of Lords. The second Home Rule Bill was primarily designed to give the responsibility for settling the land question to an Irish 'local' parliament. Gladstone retired the following year. With him and Parnell gone, the unionists consolidated and with nationalist Ireland racked and split by the Parnell controversy, the Home Rule movement seemed lost. Nationalist morale receded once again.

The separatists in these years were a tiny majority. The IRB was the main republican organisation. It was small and disorganised. James Connolly, an independent socialist, formed the Irish Socialist Republican Party in 1896. It was even smaller, without any national network and minus the support, moral and material, which the IRB received from Clan na Gael in the USA. Connolly was a supreme propagandist and prolific writer. He argued constantly and vigorously that the national and social struggles were one. His was a voice in the wilderness.

Elsewhere there were small stirrings. Dr Douglas Hyde was a scholar and a poet. He was no revolutionary but he profoundly regretted the destruction of Irish literature and language. In 1893 he founded the Gaelic League. The following year, Michael Cusack started the Gaelic Athletic Association. A ripple, then a wave of enthusiasm swept the country. The Irish language was learned and taught, music, dance and games revived, and ballads written.

A people so long repressed and despised that they almost believed the propaganda about their inferiority embraced their newly discovered culture with pride. W.B. Yeats, Lady Gregory, Synge, Maud Gonne and George Russell revived and performed ancient sagas.

Few of those involved realised how seditious these activities really were. National regeneration was bound to challenge the status quo. Yet that was not the intention nor could the widespread success of these activities be foreseen by their founders. It was ten years later that Pearse wrote: 'The Gaelic League will be recognised as the most revolutionary influence that has ever come to Ireland'. But for nationalist Ireland in 1898 there seemed no opening anywhere for activity more effective than talking at Westminster, writing and debating for Ireland (in Irish or English), singing Gaelic songs, staging dramas or playing games.

In 1898 Arthur Griffith, later founder of Sinn Féin, started a weekly newspaper, *The United Irishman*. Griffith was not a republican but his newspaper was to provide an important focus for political debate.

In the same year Thomas Clarke was released from prison in England. It was the year of the centenary of the United Irishmen. Clarke was an IRB man. He had just served over fifteen years in jail. He was persuaded to reorganise the IRB.

The IRB's strength and weakness was its secrecy. It was interested in every Irish organisation that could further the cause of Irish independence. Such organisations often became the object of its influence and sometimes of its secret control. Clarke turned his attention and the attention of his colleagues to the organisations which had sparked off and sustained the national revival. They were to discover that their republican ideas had a responsive and receptive audience, throughout Ireland and including Belfast.

2. The North began

The North began, the North held on,
The strife for native land;
When Ireland rose to smite her foes
God bless the Northern land.

Thomas Davis

In the 1790s Belfast was the centre of an Irish political movement which linked Antrim and Down with the Republics of France and America, and Belfast citizens celebrated the Fall of the Bastille, drank toasts to Mirabeau and Lafayette and studied Paine's great book, *The Rights of Man.* Presbyterians formed the Society of United Irishmen and declared for Catholic emancipation, for the abolition of church establishments and tithes, for resistance to rack-rents and for sweeping agrarian reforms. They gave a cordial welcome to Mary Wollstonecraft's *Vindication of the Rights of Women* and joined with their Catholic neighbours in the struggle for national independence and political democracy.

Yet within two generations, the majority of Presbyterians had completely abandoned their revolutionary principles, embraced the politics of the Tories and developed a deep-rooted antipathy towards their Catholic neighbours. This transformation was caused directly by the forces of reaction, supported by the wealthy landlord class who feared the union of Protestant, Catholic and Dissenter.

By the beginning of the 20th century, Belfast was becoming a major industrial city. Its industries depended on Britain for its markets and they began to share the benefits of an expanding empire.

The 'prosperity' of the region around Belfast was primarily the produce of its shipbuilding and repairing industry, which in turn owed its existence to the English capitalist classes which fostered the rise of Belfast because it suited their economic and their class interests.

The economic gap between Ulster and the rest of Ireland was widening as Belfast came to represent more than ever an outpost of industrialised Britain in Ireland. It was cheaper to transport goods by sea to Glasgow or Liverpool than to send them by train to Dublin.

The predominantly Protestant businessmen and merchants were strong supporters of the Union. Belfast's Catholics had little share in this commercial and industrial expansion and identified with the majority of the Irish population. While Belfast mushroomed, more Catholics came to look for work and were seen by unionists as a threat to their jobs, especially in times of recession.

The Ulster unionists cemented the Orange link and secured the allegiance of Protestant workers by a systematic policy of discrimination against Catholic workers, which left the Protestants with a virtual monopoly of the well-paid, skilled trades. As the Home Rule campaign intensified, the influence of the Orange Order was increased by the growing sectarian tension in Belfast. Despite this hostile atmosphere, the national revival which swept the rest of the country flourished in Belfast also. The wave of national regeneration saw the spread of the GAA and the Gaelic League, the establishment of the Ulster Literary Theatre and the performance of Yeats' *Cathleen Ni Houlihan* in the city.

Belfast republicans played a pivotal role in these activities. In those days they were a small minority. Indeed, for some time the republican standard had been kept aloft through the efforts of two outstanding women, Alice Milligan and Ethna Carberry, who produced a small but influential separatist periodical, *An Shan Van Vocht*. As the general situation developed, they were to become a catalyst for other activists.

These included: Denis McCullough from Divis Street in west Belfast, who went on to become President of the IRB and the Belfast commandant of the Volunteers; Bulmer Hobson from Holywood, County Down, who was to swear Patrick Pearse into the IRB; Roger Casement from County Antrim, who was hanged by the British for treason in 1916; Seán MacDiarmada from Country Leitrim, who was to be a signatory of the 1916 Proclamation; Eoin MacNéill, who was to give the countermanding order at that fateful time; and Winifred Carney, secretary to James Connolly and one of the last fighters to leave the GPO in Dublin after the Rising was crushed.

MacDiarmada, McCullough and Hobson played major roles in the revitalisation of republicanism in Belfast. When they first became involved in politics at the turn of the century, the Irish Parliamentary Party was in the ascendant and the republicans were a small, isolated group.

The Irish Republican Brotherhood (IRB) in the city was made up mostly of old Fenians who appeared to be more concerned with drinking and reminiscing than with revolution. In 1901, Denis McCullough was sworn into the IRB in Donnelly's public house at Omar Street on the Falls Road. Although initially disenchanted by this introduction to 'the organisation', McCullough commenced to recruit young men into new IRB circles and began a process of phasing out the older men and tightening up internal discipline.

He reorganised the Belfast IRB so effectively that in 1908 he was co-opted to the Supreme Council; he was elected Ulster representative from 1901 to 1916, becoming President of the Council in December 1915. Born in 1883 and educated by the Christian Brothers, he joined with Bulmer Hobson in forming the Dungannon Clubs, an open debating and literary society which issued a national manifesto in 1905 and grew to a strength of fifty in Belfast, campaigning against recruitment for the British Army and printing many leaflets and postcards which sold widely throughout the country.

Bulmer Hobson was born in Holywood, County Down, and moved to Belfast to a job in a printing works. His family were Quakers and his father a Gladstonian Home Ruler. At the age of twelve he became a subscriber to *An Shan Van Vocht*, the separatist

Seán MacDiarmada

nationalist periodical edited by Alice Milligan and Ethna Carberry, with whom he was to become acquainted. Influenced by these ladies and by the literary revival of that time, Hobson assisted Maud Gonne MacBride in organising a '98 centenary commemoration which led to the performance of Yeats' *Cathleen Ni Houlihan* in Belfast and the subsequent use of theatre for nationalist propaganda.

He joined the Gaelic League and the fledgling Gaelic Athletic Association (GAA) and in 1900 founded the Ulster Debating Society for Boys, an openly non-sectarian and nationalist association which was succeeded by the Protestant National Association, whose main aim was to recruit young Protestants for the national movement.

With David Parkhill, Hobson formed the Ulster Literary Theatre in Clarence Place, which produced plays with an Ulster flavour on political and social conditions. They were joined by such writers as Rutherford Mayne, Lynn Doyle, George Shiel and Harry Morrow of *Thompson in Tir na n-Og* fame and were successful enough to have Mayne's *The Drone* played in the Opera House.

In 1904 Denis McCullough swore Hobson into the IRB and their combined efforts were directed towards the strengthening of that organisation and towards the politicisation of the citizens of Belfast through the Dungannon Clubs and their newspaper, The Republic, which Hobson edited from an office in Royal Avenue. *The Republic* merged six months later with *The Peasant* in Dublin.

In the summer of 1905, Seán MacDiarmada arrived in Belfast from County Leitrim. MacDiarmada came to Belfast to join his brother Dan who worked in McGlade's Bar. Seán started work as a conductor on the Belfast tramways system and lived in Butler Street in Ardoyne. In those days Belfast, rather than Dublin, was the most populous city in Ireland and many people seeking employment were attracted here from the north-west of the country. The Great Northern and Sligo-Leitrim railways made Leitrim part of the Belfast hinterland, resulting in many Leitrim people being employed in factories and business houses.

MacDiarmada, who came from a republican family, soon became involved with Belfast's republican politics and with the new Sinn Féin association, representing Belfast Sinn Féin at the 1906 convention. In 1907 he became a full-time organiser for the Dungannon Clubs which amalgamated with Griffith's Cumann na nGael as the Sinn Féin League and MacDiarmada was retained as organiser with the Belfast headquarters. By this time he was a member of the IRB and had begun to organise within Sinn Féin.

This was the period during which leading activists, who were to make up the national leadership of the 1916 Rising, were starting to become acquainted with each other. For example, on December 16th 1904, Pearse made one of his many visits to Belfast for a meeting about the Irish language in St Mary's Hall. He stayed with a friend of his, Mrs Hutton of 8 Deramore Park, Malone Road. At that time Pearse was the editor of *An Claidheamh Soluis*. The speech he gave at the meeting dealt with the importance of education. He referred to American methods and ideals in education and stressed that education was not only

James Larkin

to build up a good character, but also to teach one's own history and language.

> Irish history and language should be taught as a matter of common sense and justice to every Irish boy and girl.

Meetings such as this were an obvious gathering point for republicans and other progressive elements. At the time of this meeting Pearse was a Home Ruler. Nine years later, with the obvious failure of that movement, he joined the IRB. He was sworn in by Hobson. MacDiarmada, McCullough and Hobson all played a major part in the revitalisation of republicanism in Belfast. A lot of their work was done on the Falls Road with public meetings usually being held after confraternity meetings, when the crowds streamed out of Clonard Monastery and down to the Falls Road. Seán MacDiarmada probably addressed his first public meeting outside St Paul's Chapel at the Cavendish Street/Falls Road corner when he reluctantly took the place of an absent speaker. (Cavendish Street and Cavendish Square, incidentally, were called after Lord Cavendish, the British Secretary General of Ireland, who was killed in Dublin's Phoenix Park by the Invincibles in 1882.) For a time they borrowed a contraption for showing slides from Francis Joseph Bigger and toured the Falls Road's back streets with this novel device, trailing it behind them on a cart, whose owner refused to lend his horse for fear of trouble arising in the area.

Such trouble was expected not from unionist elements but from over-zealous supporters of Joe Devlin, who was elected MP for the Falls Division in 1906. There was bitter rivalry between Devlinites and republicans which led in later years to clashes between the groups. Devlin was a leading member of the Irish Parliamentary Party (IPP) and one of the foremost supporters of John Redmond.

There was a proliferation of republican activity in Belfast in this period and quite a lot of seditious sentiment as well. For example, in 1912, when a Freedom Club was established in Belfast, the paper, *Irish Freedom*, carried the following report.

> A meeting called for the purpose of establishing a Freedom Club was held in the Fianna Hall, 117 Victoria Street, Belfast, on the 7th of June.
>
> There was a large attendance. Donnchadha Mac Con Uladh presided, Earnan de Blaghd acted as secretary.
>
> They wished it to be clearly understood at the very outset that their ideal was the establishment of an Irish republic.
>
> Seaghan Mac An Leastair made the remark that ultimately this aim should be backed by modern rifles and automatic pistols.
>
> The following resolution was passed unanimously:
>
> 'That a club to be called the Freedom Club be formed (1) to work for the establishment of an independent Irish Republic; (2) to justify and prepare for the use of every means, passive and aggressive, to attain that end; (3) to take immediate steps to extend the circulation and influence of *Irish Freedom*.'
>
> The following officers were appointed: President: Donnachada Mac Con Uladh; Vice President: Cathal Ua

Dunville Park, looking towards the Royal Victoria Hospital and Grosvenor Road, early 1900s.

Seamain; Committee: Seosamh Ó Connghalaigh, Pádraig Mac Alain, Seahgan O'Sullivan, Earnan de Blaghd, Seaghan Mac An Leastair.

The idea behind the Freedom Clubs was to organise an intellectual base for nationalists, to give them a united and articulate voice. Just over a year after this meeting, a Young Republican Party was formed. Again the proceedings were faithfully reported in *Irish Freedom* of November 1913.

Republican meetings in Belfast

18.10.1913: the banner of the Young Republican Party was unfolded. A Tricolour with an orange sunburst on a green field with white lettering inscribing the name and motto: Young Republican Party – Dia agus an Pobul.

Prior to a series of street meetings, three indoor meetings will be held in the Freedom Club, McGuinness Building, Berry Street.

Members of the new party were drawn from the ranks of the Gaelic League, the Freedom Club, the Fianna and some working-class organisations in Belfast.

Purpose: the teaching of nationality and republicanism amongst the young.

Cumann na mBan – the women's auxiliary movement – was also active in Belfast along with Fianna Eireann.

Cumann na mBan was established on April 5th 1914, and its inaugural meeting that day was held in Wynne's Hotel in Dublin. The aim of the organisation, according to its constitution, was to assist the men in the fight for freedom. Its initial appeal was to women who could give time to the establishment of the organisation, women who did not need to work.

The keynote speech of Agnes O'Farrell, who presided over that first meeting, ruled out the possibility of women taking a direct part in the fighting, except in a 'last extremity'. The women's role was to put Ireland first by helping to arm the men.

Many women elected to the Provisional Executive were relatives of leading figures in the Volunteers: Agnes Mac Néill,

St. Peter's Hill

Nancy O'Rahilly, Louise Gavan-Duffy, Mary Colum, Mrs Tuohy, Nurse McCoy, Elizabeth Bloxham and Margaret Dobbs.

Some women who refused to work in this subsidiary capacity joined the Citizen Army, while others ignored any statute which restricted their role.

There is no record of any Citizen Army organisation in Belfast, though many of the leading women activists, including Countess Markievicz, were members of the women's section of the Citizen Army. Connolly's influence was also important in achieving a fair measure of acceptance of women as comrades-in-arms.

On August 15th 1915, when Jeremiah O'Donovan Rossa was buried in Dublin and Pearse made his famous speech at the graveside, a Cumann na mBan activist from Belfast, Eilís Ní Chorra remembers:

> The Belfast Volunteers had organised a special train to take a crowd to Dublin for the funeral and we jumped at the chance to get away from the 'loyal' atmosphere of Belfast.

She also recalls later in 1915 a céilí being held in one of the restaurants of Belfast. It was used as a cover for a meeting of IRB officers, including Seán Mac Diarmada.

One meeting of the Belfast branch of Cumann na mBan addressed by Miss Una O'Byan, MA had over a hundred members present. In a very able lecture she analysed women's position in the home, school, business and wherein lay her duties in the welfare of the nation. A keen discussion followed in which Mrs Johnston, Miss Connolly, Mrs Gordon and others participated.

The Belfast Cumann na mBan did not confine itself to those pursuits. Its activities included first aid, stretcher-bearing, drill, signalling and rifle practice. The most proficient shots in any section of the Cumann na mBan were from the Belfast branch. Regular open-air rifle practice – Sundays at 11 a.m. – occasionally on the Divis Mountains for longer-range practice, insured this. These women felt confident enough to challenge the local Volunteers to a handicapped shooting competition. Winifred Carney, later Connolly's secretary in the GPO, came first in one of the competitions.

Nora Connolly was a principal organiser of the Belfast branch. She and her comrades were determined to ensure that women were given the same opportunities as men. In many ways the women's organisations were more progressive than the men's, especially on the national question. For example, Cumann na mBan rejected Redmond's war policy and, contrary to what happened in the National Volunteers, only a few members left over this decision.

Cumann na mBan also helped to raise the money to buy guns, including those landed by the nationalists at Howth. Connolly's daughters, Nora and Ina, of the Belfast branch of Cumann na mBan, were asked to help to smuggle some of these weapons into Belfast. A Fianna member drove the car and the two young women sat on the guns for the entire journey until they arrived safely in Belfast.

The Fianna (Fianna Éireann) has an interesting early history in Belfast. At the turn of the century the Gaelic League was very popular in the city. There were 26 branches, including the Tir na n-Og Branch based in Shaun's Park on the Whiterock Road in west Belfast. This Tir na n-Og Branch invited Michael Cusack, founder of the GAA, to come to Belfast to set up the Association in Ulster. In 1901 they started playing hurling in the Falls Park and then became embroiled in a dispute about whether RIC men were excluded from membership. Shortly after this, Bulmer Hobson, who was secretary of the first County Antrim Board of the GAA, attempted to develop a junior league, and when the Board showed little interest, he resigned and convened a meeting of boys from the Falls Road area. About three hundred attended and it was decided to form a new youth organisation, Fianna Éireann. Hobson rented Shaun's Park, and Francis Joseph Bigger presented a special trophy for the new junior league. The fledgling Fianna organisation eventually ran into financial difficulties but later, in 1909, Hobson restarted it in Dublin with the help of Countess Markievicz. Incidentally, in 1913 the Belfast Gaelic League supported the families of workers 'locked out' in Dublin and the IRB also supported the workers during Belfast's own labour dispute.

3. The cause of Ireland

The cause of labour is the cause of Ireland.
The cause of Ireland is the cause of labour.

James Connolly

As the Belfast linen industry continued to develop and ancillary industries such as engineering, brick-making, shipbuilding and rope-making sprang up, every effort was made to ensure that skilled jobs and management positions did not fall to Catholic workers. These efforts, part of a policy aimed at dividing the working people and protecting the ascendancy position of the unionist élite, were highly successful.

There had been some attempts to organise mill-workers at the turn of the century, but one of the first concerted efforts to organise trade unions among unskilled workers – unions for tradesmen and craftsmen existed in Belfast to some degree from 1788 – came in 1907 when James Larkin arrived in Belfast as organiser, even in a rudimentary form, of the National Union of Dock Labourers to organise a trade union for dock labourers, carters and coal-fillers at Belfast docks. For a brief period sectarian divisions were set aside and working people united into an effective labour movement. This unity was met by the combined opposition of the employers and the civil authorities, in most cases one and the same people, and by the RIC and the British Army. The unionist press, politicians and employers did their utmost to undermine Larkin's influence by denouncing him as a 'socialist and a Catholic' and by warning Protestant workers not to join the labour agitations. In May, a lockout of union men at the Belfast docks led to a strike which quickly spread to other workplaces when blackleg and scab labour was imported from Liverpool by the employers.

Thousands of extra RIC and British soldiers were drafted into the city to protect the strike-breakers and the employers stated that 'no person representing any trade union or combination' would be recognised by them, they would exercise the right to employ or dismiss whom they chose, and that if a strike took place without three days' written notice, the strikers would be locked out and their jobs given to others. Every worker who wanted his job back was given until July 15th to sign a document accepting these conditions. The document was rejected.

The workers remained united, despite frenzied efforts by the establishment to divide them, especially during the mad month of July, and those on strike were supported by other workers, including the Belfast Trades Council, the Belfast branches of the Amalgamated Society of Carpenters and Joiners, the Belfast railwaymen and the linen workers. Larkin's efforts were also supported by the Dungannon Clubs, whose prominent members in Belfast, Denis McCullough, Bulmer Hobson, Robert Lynd and Seán MacDiarmada, actively supported the strikers.

By the end of July the strike involved two and a half thousand dockers, coal-fillers and carters and had even spread to the ranks of the RIC. The near mutiny in that force, despite the dismissal of the chief spokesman, Constable Barrett, and the transfer of other dissidents, forced the government to improve pay and conditions for RIC men.

In August, in an effort to provoke sectarian violence, extra troops were stationed in west Belfast with the express purpose of provoking clashes between them and local people. Parts of the Falls were cordoned off and residents were stopped, searched and questioned. This harassment led to demonstrations and riots until, on August 12th, the troops opened fire on a crowd of Catholics assembled on the Grosvenor Road. Two people were killed and many others were seriously injured. Larkin, who was on the Falls Road during this period, denounced, with local labour leaders, the presence of British troops in such force in the Falls area when the strike was taking place in another part of town.

The unionist newspapers used the shooting to portray the labour agitation as 'part of a conspiracy against the unionist cause in Ireland'.

The British trade union leaders became alarmed and rushed to Belfast where they commenced talks with the employers without any consultation with Larkin. They agreed on a pay increase and on the right of the employers to employ non-union labour. The strike ended on August 28th and Larkin was later to claim that the men were forced back by the unions' refusal to continue paying them strike pay. Although the alliance of Protestant and Catholic workers only temporarily united these divided sections of the working people, it showed very clearly what could be achieved if a permanent unity could be forged; but it was also clear how remote, given the influence of Orangeism, such a development really was within a society dominated by the Orange ascendancy.

These efforts to organise the dock workers and carters into a united, even if temporary, labour movement in 1907 had left the Belfast linen workers largely untouched, and by 1911 new rules forbidding singing or laughing were introduced in the mills. Women could be fined for such 'offences' or for fixing their hair during working hours, and the penalty for bringing a newspaper, darning or knitting needles to work was instant dismissal.

It was women and children who worked in these mills, while men were generally employed as unskilled workers, carters or building labourers. Because of the consistently high level of male unemployment, women, with regular work in the mills, became the breadwinners. They were employed for a minimum wage, slaving from 6.30am to 6pm; on Saturdays work stopped at noon. The flax had to go through nine different processes, all extremely dangerous to workers' health; and for this the women at the turn of the century earned some eight shillings a week.

James Connolly

Children, mostly girls, worked for the same hours as the adults, until new legislation in 1874 introduced an arrangement whereby one week they worked three days and went to school the other two, and the following week the balance was reversed. These children were called half-timers. In 1891 the minimum age for mill-workers was raised to eleven and in 1901 to twelve. Half-timers in the years 1904-7 were paid 3s. $4\frac{1}{2}$d. for the 'long week' and 2s. $11\frac{1}{2}$d. for the 'short week'.

The working conditions in the mills were worse even than the living conditions in the small back streets. In the spinning rooms, the uncomfortably hot air was kept damp to prevent the fine linen thread from breaking and in the earlier stages of the process, the very air in the carding or spinning rooms was thick with fine 'pouce' or dust which came from the raw flax. The mill-workers and especially the doffers, who worked barefooted, inhaled this pouce and serious bronchial illness was common. The death rate from tuberculosis was also very high, with the result that greater numbers of these workers died before the age of forty-five and children were generally small and badly developed. In 1897 an outbreak of typhoid affected some twenty-seven thousand people. Long hours in such conditions and an inadequate diet of tea, buttermilk, potatoes, herrings, cheap cuts of meat and a variety of home-baked bannocks and farls did little to alleviate such consistent ill-health.

In 1909, Dr Bailie, City Medical Officer of Health, stated in an official report:

> Premature births were found to be most prevalent among women who worked in the mills and factories, engaged in such work as the following – spinning, weaving, machining, tobacco-spinning and laundry work. Many of the women appear to be utterly unable for such work owing to the want of sufficient nourishment and suitable clothing and being through stress of circumstances compelled to work to the date of confinement would be accountable for the many young and delicate children found by the Health Visitors.

Dr Bailie also recorded:

> As in previous years it is found that consumption [pulmonary tuberculosis] is most prevalent among the poor, owing largely to the unfavourable conditions under which necessity compels them to live such as dark, ill-ventilated houses and insanitary habits together with insufficient food and clothing.

A Belfast street song still heard today reflects on that period and on how marriage provided a possible, if temporary, escape.

Wallflower, wallflower, growing up so high,
All the little children are all going to die,
All except for Kathy McKay for she's the only one,
She can dance, she can sing,
She can show her wedding ring.

The working regime in the mills was extremely harsh. If you were late, you lost a day's work with the subsequent hardship caused by the loss of wages. The workers were summoned to their toil by the penetrating screech of the mill-horn which wakened the slumbering populace at 5 a.m. The women were unorganised, as were most of the working people, and any attempt to improve conditions or assert their right to belong to trade unions met with united opposition from the employers.

In 1911, James Connolly came to Belfast and the Falls Road. He had been invited back to Ireland, from America, by the Socialist Party of Ireland and promised a wage of £2 a week. He joined the newly formed Irish Transport and General Workers' Union. [The union was founded by James Larkin in January 1909 as the Irish Transport Workers' Union, but by 1911 it was known as the Irish Transport and General Workers' Union and, at the suggestion of William O'Brien, the words 'and General' were formally added to its title at the beginning of 1912.] In July 1911, Connolly was appointed Ulster organiser and secretary. Moving to Belfast to take up the post, he had to split his family up amongst republican and socialist friends around the city while he stayed with his friend Danny McDevitt at 5 Rosemary Street, until he found a home to rent.

His £2 a week was rarely paid, so that his friends D.R. Campbell, Danny McDevitt and Joe Mitchell pawned their gold watches to pay the first instalment of rent and buy groceries. The house was at 1 Glenalina Terrace, now 420 Falls Road, just below and opposite the City Cemetery, facing the Whiterock Road.

When Connolly came to Belfast, Home Rule was once again on the cards and the antagonism between the two sections of the working class was at one of its periodical peaks. This was heightened by the divisions among trade unionists. Connolly's union, the ITGWU, was regarded as a 'Fenian' breakaway. Only seven members turned up at its first Belfast branch meeting.

Later a proposal to establish an Irish Labour Party was countered by a motion from William Walker pledging support for the British Labour Party. This difference of opinion is reflected in the interesting and still relevant debate between Connolly and Walker on these and related issues.

It was obviously hardly the time to repeat Larkin's success of working class union but, against all the odds, Connolly set about the job of organising and winning recognition of the labour unions, especially in the docks. Despite all the difficulties he managed to bring out the largely Catholic deep-sea dockers in sympathy with the predominantly Protestant cross-channel seamen. He also managed to arrange the unusual spectacle of a non-sectarian 'labour band' parading through the streets.

When Connolly organised the predominantly Protestant aluminium workers into the ITGWU it inevitably involved a strike for recognition. The following Sunday, the strikers were invited to stay behind after the normal church service whereupon they received a sermon from the clergy on the evil of their actions and, more important, on the Irishness of Connolly's union. The strike was nothing but a Papish plot, they were told. Next day the men returned to work.

Similar problems arose because Connolly's activities in organising and seeking improvement for lower paid workers threatened the craft differentials enjoyed by Protestant workers. This became evident when he tried to organise the women workers in Belfast's linen mills.

The strike ended in compromise, and according to the *Irish News* of October 6th 1911, Mr. Joseph Devlin, the MP for Belfast, 'secured a special committee to investigate labour conditions in the mill.' The details of this strike by the 'slaves of slaves' makes interesting reading. It occurred at a time when the mill owners had agreed after a lot of agitation, and much publicity work about conditions by Connolly, to limit production by 15%. In practice, however, each manufacturer attempted to maintain production at the same level while working shorter hours. This was done by speeding up the machinery and thus increasing the workload upon the mill workers. They, frustrated by the lack of action from their own union leaders, soon turned to Connolly for help.

Motorised Division of the UVF

Nora Connolly, James Connolly's daughter) describes a meeting in Connolly's office in Corporation Street:

> 'Yes', a woman near the fire was saying, her husky voice fierce and bitter, 'it's over forty-five years since I started working in the mills. I was just turned eight when I began. When you were eight you were old enough to work. Worked in the steam, making your rags all wet and sometimes up to you ankles in water. The older you got the more work you got. If you got married you kept on working. Your man didn't get enough for a family. You worked 'til your baby came and went back as soon as you could; and then, God forgive you! you counted the days 'til your child could be a half-timer and started the whole hell of a life over again.

It wasn't long until the women were driven out on strike. On October 1911 over a thousand of them marched out of various mills and appealed to Connolly to lead them. He readily gave his support, although the Textile Operatives Society representatives refused to give theirs and advised the women not to strike. Without union funds to back them the women could draw only two shillings a week strike pay which they secured by street collections. Connolly wrote:

> Girls fought heroically. We held a meeting in St Mary's Hall and packed it with three thousand girls and women. They were packed from floor to ceiling, squatting on the floor between the platform and the seats – three thousand cheering, singing enthusiastic females and not a hat among them.

At such a meeting on the Custom House steps, Nora Connolly spoke in public for the first time.

The strike was essentially about conditions; while Connolly had put a demand for higher pay he regarded this as a negotiating point which could be given in return for an improvement in working conditions so that 'should any girl feel happy enough to sing, she can do so without any fear of losing her job'. Yet despite all their efforts, it soon became clear that the strikers were being beaten by the lack of union funding, some clerical opposition and the powerful position of the mill owners. They were in no position to win their demands by orthodox methods, and solidarity was crumbling. In fact, only two mills were affected by the strike and neither of these – York Street Flax Spinning Company and Milewater Mills – were on the Falls Road. The majority of women were so oppressed that Connolly's attempt to free 'the linen slaves' was well nigh impossible. *The Irish News* perhaps best summed up the 'respectable' nationalist attitude when it offered the opinion that 'unorganised displays of this kind can lead to no industrial gain for the workers and can only serve to prejudice their position'. The strike was also attacked by some Catholic priests.

Furthermore, with a surplus of linen, the mill-owners could afford to lock out and starve the strikers while the Textile Operatives' Society, opposed to Connolly's republican views, persistently attacked him. Two weeks after the strike began Connolly proposed that the women commence a 'stay-in-strike', one of the first examples of the use of this tactic in Ireland. He advised the women to go back 'but not in ones and twos, but gather outside the mills and all go in in a body and go in singing. Defy every oppressive and unreasonable rule. If one girl laughs and is reproved let everyone laugh. If a girl is checked for singing let the whole room start singing at once and if any one is dismissed, all should put on their shawls and march out. And when you are returning march in singing and cheering.'

And so, in some cases at least, it came to be. One manager who sent a girl home had to send for her again. Work was resumed only when she returned and was welcomed back with a song. Though the strike had failed, a moral victory was gained. About three hundred doffers and spinners were organised into the Irish Textile Workers' Union, a section of the ITGWU, and Connolly helped them to satisfy their need for recreation by renting a small hall in the Falls Road as a club and engaging a fiddler and a teacher of Irish dancing. The women helped to pay for this by a small weekly subscription and all enjoyed 'the Mills Girls' Ball', which was held every year, as well as an excursion to the country or seaside. And in return the mill girls made up a song about Connolly.

Cheer up Connolly, your name is everywhere,
You left old Blady sitting in the chair,
Crying for mercy, mercy wasn't there,
So cheer up, Connolly, your name is everywhere.

Drawing largely on his Belfast experience, Connolly, in December 1911, was to write of 'a discontented working class and a rebellious womanhood. I cannot separate these two great things in my mind. Every time the labourer, be it man or woman, secures a triumph in the baffle for juster conditions, the mind of the labourer receives that impulse towards higher things that comes from the knowledge of power [...] the fruits of victory of the organised working class are as capable of being stated in terms of spiritual uplifting as in the material terms of cash'.

And in the *The Reconquest of Ireland* (1915) Connolly returned to the plight of the millworkers, vividly describing at length their working and living conditions and castigating the establishment.

> In these industrial parts of the North of Ireland the yoke of capitalism lies heavily upon the backs of the people... In this part of Ireland the child is old before it knows what it is to be young [...] In their wisdom our lords and masters often leave full grown men unemployed but they can always find use for the bodies and limbs of our children.

Connolly also opposed as best he could the sectarianism of that time not only by his efforts to unionise the working people and through his political writings but by campaigning against Orange and Green toryism. He had harsh words of the Ancient Order of Hibernians (AOH), Joe Devlin and John Redmond as well as their more powerful counterparts of the Orange Order.

Orange sectarianism had grown in the spring of 1912. By July of that year, disturbances were increasing on a daily basis. In Belfast shipyard by the Twelfth of July over two thousand Catholics were chased from their work. As tension mounted, the expulsions of Catholics spread to the ropeworks and other industries. It was while this madness was at its height that Connolly organised his 'Labour Demonstration' under the auspices of the ITGWU, 'the only union that allows no bigotry in its ranks.'

Headed by the Non-Sectarian Labour Band, a procession of dockers and mill workers left 122 Corporation Street at 7.45 p.m. and walked to Cromac Square via Victoria Street, Edward Street and Cromac Street. From then on, labour demonstrations became a regular weekly event in Belfast, usually in Library Street. Civil and religious liberty and women's suffrage were the most frequent subjects. In January 1913 Connolly unsuccessfully contested Dock Ward in the municipal elections. By now he was a delegate to the Belfast Trades Council and he was supported in the election by this body. He had founded the Irish Labour Party the year before and during the Great Lock-Out of 1913, he went to Dublin to help Larkin to direct the strike and later replaced him when Larkin was imprisoned. When the Citizen Army was formed to protect the workers, Connolly threw himself into the organisation of that body. He was ably assisted by County Antrim man Jack White. The Dublin strikes ended in 1914 but the Citizen Army remained to become a central force in the build-up to, and the execution of, the Rising.

In Belfast during this period tension was steadily increasing. On his return there, Connolly found it difficult to address city centre meetings. He was confined, to a large extent, to the Falls, New Lodge and Ardoyne areas.

The increase in sectarianism and the playing of the Orange card by the Tories were matters of great concern to him. In particular, he was concerned at the possibility of partition. When it was first hinted at, he wrote:

> It is felt that the proposal to leave the Home Rule minority at the mercy of an ignorant majority with the evil record of the Orange Party is a proposal that never should have been made, and that the establishment of such a scheme should be resisted with armed force if necessary [...] Belfast is bad enough as it is; what it would be under such rule the wildest imagination could not conceive.

4. No surrender

Ulster will fight and Ulster will be right.

Randolph Churchill

The Orange Order, an exclusively Protestant and bitterly anti-Catholic organisation, was formed in 1795 to protect poorer Protestant farmers and rich Protestant landlords; it was an alliance of the landed gentry and those poorer Protestants who were united in their distrust of liberalism and Irish Catholics. Political and religious bigotry of the most extreme description were fused together and, as the power of Orangeism increased, Belfast saw the first of the riots with which we are so familiar to the present day.

Loyalism, with its bigoted and irrational hatred of Catholics and its conservative politics, has nothing to do with the Protestant religion. Due to historical circumstances the Protestant religion has been continually dragged into association with it and religion, in particular Protestantism, has been brought into disrepute by this association.

Loyalism is not based on religious consideration. Rather, it is based on power, a power which is perceived as being unsustainable without the subservience of the Catholic population. But the hatred and contempt relate clearly to the question of power, and the responsibility for this rests with the British government.

It was a political crisis in Britain which led to the playing of the Orange Card in Ireland and to the rekindling of sectarianism and the birth of modern loyalism. This occurred when the British Liberal Party commenced the democratisation of the political system in Britain by measures aimed at reducing the authority of the House of Lords over the Commons, thus curtailing the power of the British landlords and aristocrats.

The Liberals were at this time the voice of British democracy. The majority of Liberals represented the 'sensible' capitalist classes who had emerged during the industrial revolution. They had no time for aristocratic superstitions, the Divine Right of Kings or the House of Lords. The Tories, on the other hand, were interested only in preserving their political power in the British parliamentary system. They had a 'born to rule' mentality and were outraged at the erosion of their power which occurred in the latter half of the 19th century as the Liberals gradually extended voting rights to the ordinary British males.

At the same time in Ireland the Home Rule movement, led by Parnell, was steadily gaining ground. The Home Rule movement was not separatist or republican and it had the support of the British Liberal Party from 1872.

It was the third Home Rule Bill of 1912 which was to be the test of wills between the Tories and the Liberals. The Liberals had passed the Parliament Act which curtailed the power of the Tory-dominated House of Lords. Before this the Lords had the power to veto any act carried in the Commons. Now they could only delay a Bill or Act passed by the Commons.

The Home Rule Bill became a rallying point for Tory discontent. Fearful of the consequences for the British class system if they organised against the Liberals on 'British' issues, the Tories choose Ireland as the battlefield and Home Rule as the issue. They could not defeat democracy in Britain so they homed in on the anti-democratic spirit of Orangeism in north-east Ulster as a means of disrupting the advance towards democracy in Britain itself.

The main leadership of the opposition to Home Rule was provided by British Tories who now championed and instigated a reactionary movement in the north of Ireland. They found willing allies there. Edward Carson, a Dublin man, one time Solicitor-General, at this time a member of the Privy Council and a Conservative MP for Dublin University, became the leader of this 'loyal' movement.

Their campaign against the British parliament was launched in September 1911 at Craigavon, the home of James Craig. Over one hundred thousand Orangemen assembled there to pledge themselves against Home Rule. Two days later notice was given that an Ulster Unionist Council was prepared to take control of that area if Home Rule was introduced.

The garrison class, as they are described by Dorothy MacArdle, was apprehensive of finding itself reduced from the status of a privileged ascendancy to the position of a national minority. Their British allies exploited that fear.

Lord Randolph Churchill declared that the Orange Card was the card to play and prayed that it would turn up trumps. Tories rallied to the cause to defeat the 'tyranny of the Commons' and provided the training and guns for the Ulster Volunteer Force (UVF) which was established with the help of Sir Henry Wilson, Chief of the British Imperial General Staff. Weapons were stored not only in Orange Halls in Belfast, but in Tory Clubs in Britain as well.

Inflammatory speeches by Tory leaders led to sectarian riots in Belfast and to attacks on Catholic workmen in Belfast shipyards, and as the temperature rose, the UVF continued to arm itself. During September 1912 a great series of unionist demonstrations took place and the Ulster Covenant was launched.

> 'I am told it [a Provisional Ulster Government] will be illegal', Carson declared. 'Of course it will. Drilling is illegal [...] the Volunteers are illegal [...] Don't be afraid of illegalities.'

Later that year the Ulster Unionist Council resolved itself into the Central Authority of the Provisional Government of Ulster. At that time the province of Ulster was represented at Westminster by seventeen nationalists and sixteen unionists. Ulster could scarcely be described as unionist.

Yet the Liberals did nothing to suppress this Tory conspiracy. They reasoned that if they confronted the Tories the fledgling

British Labour Party would exploit the situation and encourage a class war in Britain, in which the Liberals as well as the Tories might perish.

The climax of the Tory revolt occurred in 1914 when 57 British Army officers resigned after being ordered to put down the revolt, and this Curragh Mutiny, as it was called, broke the nerve of the Liberal Party.

By this time negotiations had already started between the British government, the unionist and nationalist parties to exclude six counties of Ulster from Home Rule. Redmond, Parnell's lesser successor, agreed to allow some Ulster counties to opt out of the putative Irish parliament for a period of six years. When this first hint of partition became public knowledge, nationalist Ireland was unanimous in its opposition.

> 'To even discuss', said Sinn Féin, 'the exclusion of Ulster or any portion of Ulster from a Home Rule measure is in itself traitorous [...] So long as England is strong and Ireland is weak, England may continue to oppress this country; but she shall not dismember it.

'If this nation is to go down,' wrote Irish Freedom, 'let it go down gallantly as becomes its history, let it go down fighting, but let it not sink into the abjectness of carving a slice out of itself and handing it over to England [...] As for Ulster, Ulster is Ireland's and shall remain Ireland's. Though the Irish nation in its political and corporate capacity were gall and wormwood to every unionist in Ulster yet shall they swallow it.

> We will fight them if they want fighting; but we shall never let them go, never.

Sinn Fein and the republicans were no more emphatic than the Labour Party. James Connolly in the *Irish Worker* said of partition:

> To it Labour should give the bitterest opposition, against it. Labour in Ulster should fight even to the death if necessary as our fathers fought before us.

Connolly even used the menace of partition as an argument in favour of joining the Citizen Army and urged that the Irish Volunteers, formed in November 1913 to defend Home Rule, should transfer their membership to the Citizen Army which 'meant business.' 'The Citizen Army,' he continued, 'stand for Ireland – Orange and Green – one and indivisible.'

According to R.M. Henry in *The Evolution of Sinn Féin*, Sinn Féin saw that, though partition was unacceptable, it was no use continually asking the unionists to name the safeguards they wanted. They would not name what they did not want: no safeguards would secure them in a democratic modern community against their chief objection to Home Rule – that in an Irish parliament Protestants, as such, would be in 'a permanent minority'.

It was of the very nature of things that they should be, if representative institutions were to be recognised at all. But though in a minority they need not be, as they asserted they would be, subject to disabilities, and Sinn Féin held that every offer to allay their fears compatible with free institutions should be made. A Sinn Féin Convention held in Dublin towards the end of April 1914, agreed to make the Ulstermen, on behalf of Sinn Féin, the following proposals:

1. Increased representation in the Irish parliament on the basis partly of rateable value and partly of bulk of trade, the Ulster representation to be increased by fifteen members, including one for the University of Belfast; two members to be given to the unionist constituency of Rathmines;
2. To fix all Ireland as the unit for the election of the Senate or Upper House and to secure representation to the Southern unionist minority by Proportional Representation;
3. To guarantee that no tax should be imposed on the linen trade without the consent of a majority of the Ulster representatives;
4. That the Chairman of the Joint Exchequer Board should always be chosen by the Ulster Representatives;

5. That all posts in the Civil Service should be filled by examination;
6. That the Ulster Volunteer Force should be retained under its present leaders as portion of an Irish Volunteer Force and should not, except in case of invasion, be called upon to serve outside Ulster;
7. That the Irish Parliament should sit alternately in Dublin and in Belfast;
8. That the clauses in the Home Rule Bill restricting Irish trade and finance and prohibiting Ireland from collecting and receiving its own taxes, or otherwise conflicting with any of the above proposals, should be amended.

These proposals, though approved of generally by the Belfast Trades Council, were contemptuously ignored by the Ulster unionist leaders.

The offer of partition likewise was promptly rejected by them: like the Irish Citizen Army they 'meant business'. They meant to smash Home Rule for good and all, for the South as well as for the North of Ireland, and in conjunction with the English Tories they felt strong enough to do it. They began openly to tamper with the allegiance of the army.

Not only did large numbers of ex-officers offer their services to the Ulster Volunteers, but many officers on the active list announced their intention of refusing to obey orders if despatched to preserve order in Ulster, if as broadly hinted by the unionists the UVF seized military depots in the province.

It was an open boast in Belfast that the ship conveying UVF arms from Hamburg to Ulster had been sighted, but allowed to pass unchallenged by officers of the Royal Navy on the ships detailed to intercept it.

The outbreak of the First World War intervened in all these deliberations and conspiracies. The Home Rule Bill was suspended until the end of the war.

5. The Irish Volunteers

Oh had they died by Pearse's side
Or fallen by Cahal Brugha
Their names we would keep where the Fenians sleep
'Neath the shade of the foggy dew.

Eoin MacNéill was born in Glenarm, County Antrim. He was educated at St. Malachy's College in Belfast where he was a brilliant scholar. In the Intermediate Examinations he achieved the highest place in all Ireland in the senior grades. He studied Old, Middle and Modern Irish at University College Dublin and when the Gaelic League was founded in 1893, MacNeill became its first honorary secretary.

In 1897 he was appointed the first professor of Irish in Drumcondra Teacher Training College.

An article, 'The North Began', written by him, was published in Pearse's Gaelic league paper *An Claidheamh Soluis* on November 1st 1913. It facilitated the formation of an Irish Volunteer movement.

The leaders of the IRB, ever watchful for any opportunity to advance their cause, seized this one. MacNéill was a perfect choice to front such an organisation. The O'Rahilly was delegated to approach him, without declaring the IRB interest, to establish the Volunteers.

This was done at a huge overflow meeting marshalled by the Fianna in the Rotunda in Dublin on November 25th. Four thousand men enlisted in the Volunteers that evening and Eoin MacNéill became the organisation's first president.

In his opening address he pointed out that the new organisation did not 'contemplate any hostility' to the Ulster Volunteer Force. He hoped the UVF would emulate the example of the United Irishmen.

The UVF parading in front of Belfast City Hall, 1915

It is not recorded whether his optimism was shared by his audience which represented most nationalist opinion except Redmond's Parliamentary Party. Redmond's followers were, however, to join later when the growth of the organisation was such that it was too large to be ignored. By the end of the year the Irish Volunteers were believed to be ten thousand strong and increasing daily.

Bulmer Hobson was Secretary, Casement was Treasurer, Mellows and other republicans of the Fianna were responsible for training. Patrick Pearse, Thomas MacDonagh and Joseph Plunkett were among those who took prominent roles, while behind them Thomas Clarke and the IRB's better known leaders quietly helped to build an army whose purpose for them was to be more revolutionary than that envisaged by MacNéill and others. They found willing recruits in the GAA and other Irish-Ireland organisations.

When the British government, nine days after the establishment of the Volunteers, published a proclamation prohibiting the importing of arms into Ireland, many Irish people felt that it did so with Redmond's agreement, on whose support the government depended. Nationalist opinion was not amused and the Irish Party was solemnly warned by one advanced nationalist paper.

> Mr Redmond has had his chance. When partition is again mentioned, let him stand aside even at the cost of the 'Home Rule' Bill. There is a force and a spirit growing in Ireland which in the wrangle of British politics he but vaguely realises.

But Mr Redmond was not so preoccupied with 'the wrangle of British politics' as he seemed. He realised quite clearly that the Irish Volunteers were growing in numbers and in influence and that neither their object nor their existence were compatible with the principles of Home Rule. They proclaimed their intention of putting themselves eventually at the disposal of the Irish parliament; but the British Bill contemplated a parliament which should have no right to accept their services. They were largely controlled by men who thought little of Home Rule. They were seen by him to be a menace to the success of his parliamentary policy. He decided to demand the right to nominate on the Volunteer Committee twenty-five of his followers and threatened to call those volunteers who supported him into a separate organisation unless his demands were acceded to. The committee, faced with a choice of either an open clash with Mr Redmond (a course as dangerous to them as to declare war on them would have been to him) or of submitting to his demand, decided to submit. To have permitted a split would have left the republicans without the camouflage of a wider organisation to protect them. This was crucial, especially until they procured arms. Notwithstanding this, there was severe tension within the inner circles of the IRB when the twenty five new members (four of whom were priests) joined the Committee.

This was not helped when the Citizen Army promptly criticised the reconstituted Volunteer Committee.

> 'Is there,' asked the *Irish Worker*, 'one reliable man at the head of the National Volunteer movement apart from Casement who, we believe, is in earnest and honest?
>
> 'We admit the bulk of the rank and file are men of principle and men who are out for liberty for all men; but why allow the foulest growth that ever cursed this land [the Hibernian Board of Erin] to control an organisation that might if properly handled accomplish great things?'

It accused the committee of having passed the Volunteers over to a 'gang of place-hunters and political thugs' and called upon the rank and file to sever all connection with them.

Sinn Féin was equally vehement: 'Redmond is only a tool,' it wrote, 'in the hands of Asquith and Birrell who wish to destroy the Volunteers.' *Irish Freedom* headed its leader on the transaction 'The Kiss of Judas', and declared that 'after the government the Irish Parliamentary Party in its later years has been the most evil force in Ireland.'

The original members of the Volunteer Committee, especially Casement and Hobson, were clearly under great pressure from this issue. The official position as outlined in *The Irish Volunteer*, their organ, was:

> The control of the Committee by Mr John Redmond does not matter, provided his nominees represent the feelings of the Volunteers; if they do, the Irish Party will see to the withdrawing of the Arms Proclamation and proceed to arm the Volunteers at once.

The Irish Party did neither. But the IRB had their own agenda anyway. When the Volunteers were founded The O'Rahilly was made head of a sub-committee authorised to draw upon funds secretly for weapons. A secret committee involving Casement, The O'Rahilly and Erskine Childers was also set up in London. It accepted a proposal to buy arms in Germany from Mary Spring Rice. She was assisted by Mrs Childers and Mrs Stopford Green. In July they succeeded in imitating the exploits of the unionists who had landed weapons at Donaghadee, Bangor and Larne. The Irish Volunteers ran a cargo of rifles into Howth and another was landed at Kilcool.

But the crown forces, absent from the UVF landing points, intercepted the Howth gunrunners on their way back to Dublin. They failed in their efforts to seize the weapons and on the return journey British soldiers fired upon an unarmed crowd in the streets of Dublin. The country had barely time to appreciate the contrast between Larne and Howth when the sound of the German guns in Belgium broke upon its ears.

In Belfast the rise of Irish Volunteers had been as marked as it was in other parts of the country. In fact, partially because of the unionist threat, recruiting was particularly high throughout Ulster. More than four thousand Belfast men joined in 1913.

In the west of the city the Volunteers, the Fianna and the IRB held their meetings in 'the Huts' at Beechmount. 'The Huts' covered an area above and behind where the Broadway Cinema used to stand on the Falls Road. They were originally used to billet British soldiers but were later let out as stables for local hawkers and surrounded a grassy area much used for football matches or by women playing 'housey' – the illegal forerunner of bingo.

As this programme of training published in local papers illustrates, the Volunteers were quite open about their activities.

1st West Battalion
All companies parade in Shaun's Park on Monday at 8.
2nd West Battalion
All companies parade in Shaun's Park on Thursday at 8.
North Battalion
A-Company, North Queen Street, Wednesday and Friday at 8.

B-Company, Ardoyne, on Friday at 8.
C-Company, North Queen Street, Monday and Thursday at 8.
D-Company, North Queen Street, Monday and Tuesday at 8.
E-Company, notified during week.
F-Company, Sacred Heart, North Queen Street, Friday at 8.
South and East Battalions in St. Mary's Hall on Wednesday night.

Ambulance section in St. Mary's Hall on Sunday at 3 and Wednesday at 8.
General Parade in Shaun's Park on Saturday at 4 sharp.

At the outbreak of the First World War Carson called upon the Ulster Volunteers to do battle for Britain, and Redmond made the same appeal to the Irish Volunteers. He said: 'This is a war to make the world safe for democracy and the British government will be grateful that the Irish came to its assistance'.

Twenty-nine thousand Ulster Volunteers enlisted and eighty thousand Irish Volunteers followed Redmond's advice.

Part of the Irish Volunteers denounced Redmond's authority over them and the organisation split into what became known as the National Volunteers who followed Redmond, and the Irish Volunteers who stayed with Eoin MacNéill and the separatist founders of the organisation.

When Redmond suggested that the Volunteers join the British Army, in Belfast his call was enthusiastically endorsed by Joe Devlin. For example in Lisburn, County Antrim, there were four hundred and sixty seven Volunteers. At the instigation of Devlin three hundred and sixty seven left, some in disgust, others to join the British Army. Devlin was the very popular MP for West Belfast. Like Denis McCullough, he was born in Divis Street. Educated at St Mary's Christian Brothers in Barrrack Street, Devlin was for a period the manager of Kelly's Cellars in Bank Lane, one of Belfast's oldest public houses. 'Wee Joe' as he was known, was first elected to represent North Kilkenny in 1902. In 1906 he was elected as MP for Belfast Central.

On October 25th 1914, Redmond came to Belfast where he visited Devlin's old school. In the Clonard Picture House on the

Falls Road he addressed the National Volunteers of Belfast and urged them to fight in the World War.

> If the manhood of Ireland rose up here and uniformed and drilled and armed itself, and refused to strike a blow in defence of Ireland where the real fighting is going on, believe me our country would be covered with disgrace.

Nora Connolly described his visit in a letter to her father.

> *Dear Daddie,*
> *It's a good thing you were down in Dublin these two days. You would not believe you were living on the Falls Road; you'd think some magician had taken your house and set it down on the Shankill Road. Never were there so many Union Jacks hung out to honour Sir Edward Carson as there were hung out last night and today in honour of J E Redmond. On Friday night I thought it was the limit when I saw the Union Jack on the Catholic Boys Halls along with Belgian flags; great big flags they were, and at the bottom two small threepenny green flags. I was all worked up about it but imagine my feelings when I got a little past Dunville Park on Saturday night to see a monster Union Jack, and alongside it a green banner with the inscription 'Who fears to speak of '98 […]' One AOH Division had a large Union Jack and a large green flag with a small Union Jack in the corner; underneath, a banner running the entire length of the house, with the inscription: 'We welcome the leader of the National Volunteers to Belfast'. And so it was with every AOH Division. Everywhere along the road was England's flag […] all the way from King Street to Grosvenor Road.*

Fate, however, played a hand and it rained throughout the night so that:

> In the morning their decorations, at least a good few of them, were swirling in the mud and were black with dirt […] It rained and poured all morning and never stopped raining all day. The best of it was that they had made no other arrangements, and had to send out word that the meeting was cancelled. There was still the Clonard picture house, where the women and girls were to present

> Mrs Redmond with some table linen. Poor woman, I'm sure she needs it. I do not know if any men got in there, but I heard the girls from the mills were there, so there would hardly be room for them [...].

As a result of all this fervour and a recruiting strategy which appealed separately to, and promised to fulfil the conflicting aspirations of both the Ulster and National Volunteers, three Irish Divisions were raised for the British war effort. These were the 10th, the 16th and the 36th Divisions.

Although there were exceptions, as a general rule, the 10th and the 16th Division were made up of National Volunteers, with Belfast men mostly in the 16th, and the 36th was the Ulster Division, made up of the Ulster Volunteer Force men.

Together they formed more than eighty battalions of infantry. Militarily, the whole of Ireland was administrated as a separate command directly under the British War Office. Command HQ was at Parkgate, Dublin, and on Mobilisation Day, August 4th 1914, special trains from all over Ireland travelled into the docks at Dublin, Cork and Belfast from where ships took the troops directly to France and the killing fields of Europe.

The Battle of Mons [BelgiumJ on August 23rd 1914, was the first encounter between the 'British' and the Germans.

The Second Irish Rifles suffered severely, losing three hundred men.

The Munster Fusiliers were virtually wiped out; five hundred of their men lost their lives as the Battle of Mons ended in a British retreat with a total of casualties of fifteen thousand.

A month later at the First Battle of Ypres (French Flanders) which lasted four weeks the Irish Guards lost heavily. In one day they lost almost three hundred and fifty men.

The 2nd Irish Regiment helped to take Fromelles. On October 19th, after an advance at Le Pilly they were counterattacked; very few survived. It was the same horrific story during the spring offensive of 1915. For the first time the Germans used

Eoin MacNéill

poison gas. The Irish Fusiliers lost ten officers and three hundred and fifty men in one attack.

By February the Western Front was in a stalemate and a second front was opened up in the Dardanelles, with the Battle of Gallipoli. Fighting the Turks was seen by Churchill and Lloyd George as a push-over.

It turned out to be a disastrous failure, Two hundred thousand men were killed, wounded and invalided and it achieved nothing. The 10th Division bore its share of the casualties. In August that year at the Battles of Suvla the 10th Division also lost heavily.

Again the operation turned out to be a military fiasco. The 6th Battalion of Irish Fusiliers was almost wiped out. At the end of September the 10th Division was taken out of the Peninsula to rest and regroup.

When evacuation took place on January 9th 1916, the 'British' army left thirty-eight thousand dead or missing.

At the beginning of 1916 the 'Great War' had lasted eighteen months. It had reached a deadlock.

Back home in Ireland by this time the IRB had firmly and formally committed itself to a Rising. In Belfast this presented special difficulties. Redmond advocated that the Volunteers join the British Army, the Belfast men, influenced by Joe Devlin, did so in such large numbers that after the split, only one hundred and forty-two men, including Fianna boys, plus the Cumann na mBan were left under republican control.

There were other difficulties also at national level. Not all of the Irish Volunteer leadership were in favour of a Rising and of those who were, few were in favour of an unconditional rising. The IRB worked therefore on their own, within the depleted Volunteer movement without the knowledge or permission of some of its most senior leaders, including prominent members of their own organisation. These included Bulmer Hobson and Eoin MacNéill. Despite all this by the beginning of 1916 preparations for a rising were well advanced.

6. Preparations

The best laid plans o' mice and men do oft times go astray.

Robbie Burns

Contrary to revisionist assertions and significant popular opinion, the 1916 Rising was not planned as another glorious failure. The original plan involved an elaborate uprising throughout most of the country. At one point the leaders contemplated a strategy, involving very substantial German support, which would have opened up a third front during the First World War. In 1915 Joseph Plunkett, with the help of Roger Casement, travelled to Germany on behalf of the IRB and outlined the IRB's plans to the German High Command.

The plans included:

1. The seizure of key positions throughout Ireland by republican forces.
2. An invasion force of Irish POWs from British regiments in Germany would land in Limerick from ships of the German Imperial Navy.
3. These forces would be joined by Irish American forces. (The USA had not yet entered the war.) The IRB was funded and assisted by the USA based Clan na Gael. If Germany supported Ireland and Irish Americans were part of the uprising, it was argued that this would create a pro-German sympathy in the USA, particularly among the influential American-Irish, and help to keep the USA neutral and out of the war.
4. Republican forces which seized main buildings in Dublin would hold out until relieved by the invasion forces pushing across from the west. A detailed assessment of British troop concentrations in Ireland produced by Plunkett showed that the country, and especially the west, was unprotected due to Britain's wartime commitments.
5. As the invasion and the Rising began, republican forces in other parts of the country would hamper British

> reinforcements by causing maximum damage to transport and communication networks. The viaduct at Drogheda was to be specifically targeted to prevent British troops or unionists coming south by rail.

The German High Command decided not to support the IRB to the extent that was requested, perhaps because of their critical commitments in imminent battles on the Western Front, but they did send a significant amount of arms to Ireland a year later with Roger Casement. All of this illustrates, apart from anything else, that those who were planning the Rising were not romantic fools, committed merely to blood sacrifices or gestures towards some past or future generations of Irish rebels. They were deadly serious revolutionaries, committed to their objectives of Irish independence and social transformation, and anxious to exploit by military means Britain's involvement in the World War. This is reflected even in the revised plans for the Rising.

The commitment to an armed uprising reflected also and was given an added impetus by the old Fenian adage that 'England's difficulty was Ireland's opportunity', in this case Britain's involvement in the World War.

In the 'German plan' most of the North was excluded from the national plan for the Rising. In his submission to the German High Command Plunkett gave a detailed military breakdown of each county. His analysis of the military situation in Ulster included an assessment of the unionist forces. Because of the presence of local Carson Volunteers who would mobilise in support of the British, he excluded Donegal, though he highlighted the strategic importance of its deep ports and inlets. In particular, he ruled out counties Derry, Down and Antrim, again stressing that he was only doing so because of the large presence of Carsonites. Belfast was thus effectively ruled out of his plan.

As we will see, this was also the case during the actual plan for Easter week 1916. By the beginning of that year this plan was well advanced. James Connolly was now a major influence in the republican leadership and he had begun to acquire influence over Pearse and Clarke. Gradually the concept of an insurrection conditional on a German landing, conscription or an attempt by the British to disarm the Volunteers gave way as the plan for the armed declaration of a republic took root within the IRB leadership. The British were of course, through their usual intelligence services, doing their utmost to keep an eye on the activities of the Volunteers. According to their records, in April 1916 the Volunteers were estimated to have about fifteen thousand two hundred members.

British intelligence believed that they had one thousand eight hundred and eighty-six rifles and a number of shotguns, pistols and revolvers in the provinces and approximately eight hundred and twenty-five rifles in Dublin. Distribution of arms, reported to be held by the Irish Volunteers in the city of Belfast, were: twenty-five magazine rifles; thirty-two single loaders; ten machine guns; fifty shotguns; and one hundred revolvers and pistols.

In the whole of Ulster, there were supposed to be one thousand one hundred and eighteen arms in the hands of the Irish Volunteers. The British administration knew that this was probably underestimated. It did not take into account of the theft of weapons from the Redmondite Volunteers, or the fact that many weapons were smuggled into the country, or that quite a few policemen and soldiers in British service were selling their weapons and ammunition for a good price to the Irish Volunteers.

The British were becoming increasingly worried about the activities of the republicans. In the beginning of 1915 they ordered the deportation of the main organisers of the Volunteers. Herbert W. Pim and Denis McCullough from Belfast, Liam Mellows from Wexford and Ernest Blythe from Belfast, who had both been organising in the south-west of Ireland, were ordered to leave Ireland before July 20th 1915. For failing to comply with this order McCullough was sentenced to four, and the others to three, months imprisonment. Blythe and Mellows were later deported to England.

In the week before Christmas 1915, the British Under-Secretary wrote to the Chief Secretary:

> The present situation in Ireland is most serious and menacing [...] He [Redmond] knows or should know that the enrolled strength of the Sinn Féin Volunteers has

> increased by a couple of thousand active members in the last two months […] each group of these is a centre of revolutionary propaganda. He knows or should know that efforts are being made to get arms for the support of this propaganda, that the Irish Volunteers have already some two thousand five hundred rifles, that they have their eyes on the ten thousand in the hands of the supine National Volunteers and that they are endeavouring to supplement their rifles with shotguns, pistols and revolvers.
>
> New measures, possibly requiring additional police at the ports will be required to counter these attempts and unless in other matters we keep these revolutionaries under observation, we shall not be in a position to deal with the outbreak which we hope will not occur, but which undoubtedly will follow any attempt to enforce conscription, or even if there is no such attempt, might take place as a result of continual unsuccess of the British Army.

For citizens of Belfast like everyone else, except those in the IRB leadership, the week before Easter 1916 was no different than any other year. Even among the republican or nationalist activists there was little anticipation of what lay ahead. For most of them it was to be a weekend of routine manoeuvres. For Belfast's Cumann na mBan members that meant spending a week making up endless first-aid kits in preparation for a route march on Easter Sunday. Other manoeuvres were planned for the Easter weekend.

For the Belfast Volunteers this included a train excursion to Dublin on Easter Sunday. The train was due to leave Belfast at 7.15am, to arrive in Dublin at 10.30am, and a rifle competition had been organised between the various battalions of the Dublin and Belfast Volunteers. The *Irish News* carried a notice for the Belfast Battalion to attend the Brigade Hall on the Falls Road on Holy Thursday night at 8 o'clock to pick the Belfast teams. There was to be an extra practice on Easter Saturday for the lucky competitors.

Such notices were not unusual in the newspapers of that time and manoeuvres by the various groups of armed citizens were a common occurrence. Belfast citizens, apart from those directly involved, paid little attention to these goings-on. As Easter drew near they were more interested in the coming holiday and perhaps the *Irish News* readers would have been more concerned with the special holiday programmes advertisements.

These included the screening in the Clonard Picture House, not far from the Brigade Hall on the Falls Road, of a film *The Unafraid*, while *Pygmalion* was playing down at the Grand Opera House.

For more outdoor types the weather forecast promised a pleasant weekend, a welcome boon for the fans hoping for a place in the terraces for the holiday soccer matches at Grosvenor Park, the Oval, Windsor Park and Cliftonville. It looked like being a good weekend.

Roger Casement certainly hoped so. The IRB had set Easter Sunday as the start of the Rising. It was timed for 6.30pm in Dublin and 8pm in the provinces. A shipload of arms including artillery had been dispatched from Germany. It was due to land off the Kerry coast at Banna Strand on Good Friday. Casement and Monteith were following by submarine. Six handpicked Volunteers were on their way to make contact with the arms ship and make arrangements for landing the weapons.

They included west Belfast man Charlie Monaghan who was born and reared in Arizona Street, off the Glen Road. Monaghan had a good knowledge of mechanics and wireless and had been chosen to take part in the seizing, as part of the landing operation, of the wireless station at Valentia Island. As the arms ship, the *Aud*, approached the Kerry coast everything was going according to plan.

Back in Dublin the IRB leadership was in almost continuous session. The previous few months had been eventful ones, full of feverish activity. The IRB had decided, some considerable time before, on a rising in principle. A Military Committee had busied itself drawing up plans, as we have seen, and securing arms. Casement and Plunkett had been sent to Germany and landing sites in Kerry had been examined. The leadership of the Volunteers, outside of the IRB, knew nothing of this. Neither did Connolly and he and the Irish Citizen Army were becoming increasingly impatient. He was also starting to influence rank and file activists who shared his impatience. If the IRB was to be successful it not only had to join forces with the Citizen Army, it would also have to lead out the Volunteers in defiance of their official leadership.

A meeting of the IRB's Supreme Council was summoned at Clontarf on January 16th to discuss these issues. It decided to advance from its earlier decision to organise the Rising in principle to a decision to organise it in fact. The Military Committee was empowered by this meeting to make all the necessary arrangements and to co-opt those it considered necessary.

One of the first things it did was to meet with Connolly. There could not be two leaderships or for that matter two armies or two risings. Out of that could only come chaos. Cooperation was required. The IRB decided to take Connolly into its confidence. The discussions took place on January 19th and 20th.

It is believed that Connolly told the IRB leaders, including Pearse and MacDiarmada, that the Citizen Army was planning for an unconditional rising. The IRB had already taken important policy decisions. Now it was to drop the conditions of German aid or conscription which had been considered necessary before a Rising could take place.

The January meeting agreed on an alliance between the IRB and the Citizen Army and chose April 23rd as the date for the Rising. On February 5th the date of the Rising reached Clan na nGael in the USA. The die was cast.

The British authorities had also been busy. A Fianna boy, Seamus Reader, had brought $1\frac{1}{2}$ cwt. of gelignite to Dublin from Glasgow via Belfast and Connolly's house on the Falls Road. While Connolly and the IRB met, the RIC searched for the missing explosives. Later in that month and in February and March the police activity increased, with raids on the premises of the Gaelic press and increased surveillance of the Volunteers. Some of the main organisers were arrested. Liam Mellows was among those arrested for deportation to England. He had a central role in the preparations for the Rising. Permitted to choose a place of residence in England, he chose Leek and informed his brother Barney of his choice. The IRB was anxious, so close to the Rising, to get an activist of Mellows' ability and commitment back to Ireland.

In this they had the full-hearted support of James Connolly. Connolly and MacDiarmada consulted on the matter and dispatched Barney Mellows and Nora Connolly to England via Belfast and Glasgow so that they arrived in Leek the day before Liam. They contacted him there at the Park Hotel and Barney and Liam swapped places. Liam and Nora then travelled back to Glasgow and from there back to Belfast with Liam disguised as a priest, in clothes a few sizes too big for him. Here Mellows stayed at the Connollys' house on the Falls Road while Denis McCullough arranged transport to Dublin and Nora sought clerical garments of a better fit.

When Nora Connolly and Barney Mellows travelled through England to Leek, their journey was delayed by Germany's Zeppelin raids on April 2nd and 3rd. The German war effort was hotting up. At the same time, the British were having a recruiting crisis, with not enough men enlisting. At a debate in Westminster on whether or not to bring in general conscription, the British Prime Minister Asquith was against, Edward Carson among those in favour.

Back in the north of Ireland things were hotting up also. Carson's Ulster Volunteers attacked members of the Ancient Order of Hibernians in County Armagh, near Portadown. The AOH members were building a new accommodation hall when they came under attack from some two hundred armed men of the UVF. After they had demolished the construction, the UVF men attacked nearby Catholic houses. The inhabitants had an almost miraculous escape.

Meanwhile, the *Irish News* was taking an optimistic view of the future. In an editorial criticising nationalists who opposed the payment of England's war tax, it said:

> Ireland's just share of the cost of the war should be cheerfully and willingly borne. We are bearing more than that just share and we are not threatening to smash the machinery of the state, because we are confident of our own power to secure a fair and permanent adjustment later on.

The republicans, as we have seen, had no such confidence. Key people throughout the country were being given their instructions. They included the Belfast activists. Denis McCullough, who was released from prison towards the end of 1915, was the senior IRB man in the North. When Pearse visited Belfast at the beginning of March for the Robert Emmet Commemoration, he told McCullough to be on stand-by for orders for the Rising. McCullough figured he would not be able to do much with about one hundred and thirty Volunteers, young men and boys from the Fianna, plus an unspecified number of Cumann na mBan.

The Emmet Commemoration was held in St. Mary's Hall. It was well-filled and the Volunteers provided an armed guard. According to the report in the *Workers' Republic*:

> Pearse stirred his hearers to the very depth of their souls. Never more graphically and beautifully has Emmet's story been told here. His style of speech is not such as usually appeals to a Belfast audience, but on Thursday night he held us in a spell of respectful silence. He linked up Tone and Davis with Lalor and Mitchel as the fathers of modern Irish nationalism. The public gave a standing ovation and as a result of the meeting, large numbers of men joined the Volunteers.

A month later, McCullough got orders from Connolly that when the Rising started, he and his men were to go to Tyrone, join up with the Tyrone Volunteers and then to start off to Galway to join Liam Mellows.

McCullough began to prepare urgently. He drew all the money he had from the bank – between £115 and £120 – and got Archie Heron and some of the others in the movement to purchase equipment – haversacks and various things like that – at the Ulster Volunteer Force stores. He called the section commanders together and gave them money to get their units on the train to Coalisland. He told them they were going on manoeuvres.

Within the Volunteers and the Citizen Army rumours about the pending action were gathering. Hobson, who had argued for the Volunteers to wait until after the war so that they could try to influence the peace conference, clearly suspected that a rising was imminent. But he had no proof. On the Monday before Easter, Liam Monahan came up from Limerick seeking confirmation on the actions planned for the weekend. He approached Hobson, who immediately went to Eoin MacNéill and told him his news.

Padraig Pearse

MacNéill was furious. Although it was after midnight, he went immediately to see Pearse. Pearse told him what was afoot.

'I will do everything I can to stop this except to ring the Castle', MacNéill stormed at him.

The next day, MacDonagh, MacDiarmada and Pearse succeeded in pacifying MacNéill. He agreed to do nothing for the present. Connolly and the IRB men met to consider the new situation and agreed that the Rising was still on. On Good Friday night they abducted Hobson. News of this spread rapidly and, understandably, the split in the Volunteer leadership widened.

Meanwhile, Casement's arms ship, the *Aud*, had arrived off the Kerry coast. It waited for three days and no one made contact with it. The *Aud* was captured by the British and scuttled by its crew in Cork Harbour. The news reached Dublin. Charlie Monaghan and the unit which had been sent to make contact with the *Aud* and arrange the landing had raced to their deaths, plunging off a Kerry coast road in dense fog into deep water. Casement and a comrade,

Monteith, arrived by submarine and struggled ashore to make contact with local Volunteers. Casement was arrested; Monteith got through. A local Volunteer was sent to Dublin to inform the leadership of the situation and of Monteith's advice that the Rising should be called off if it was dependent on the *Aud*. Monteith had no idea about the leadership division. He told the Volunteer to contact MacNéill or Hobson. The Volunteer contacted Connolly.

On Easter Saturday, the leadership factions met. The IRB men thought they had persuaded MacNéill that it was too late to turn back. Later that evening he went into conference with other leaders, including Arthur Griffith. After that conference MacNéill issued his famous countermanding order.

> Owing to the very critical position, all orders given to Irish Volunteers for tomorrow, Easter Sunday, are hereby rescinded, and no parades, marches, or other movements of Irish Volunteers will take place. Each individual Volunteer will obey this order in every particular.

Meanwhile, in Belfast on Easter Sunday morning, Nora Connolly and her sister joined their comrades on the train to Tyrone. Their mother had gone to Dublin with the rest of the family on Good Friday to join their father.

When the Belfast Volunteers arrived in Coalisland, they found confusion. Dr Patrick McCartan, of the Supreme Council of the IRB, was in charge. McCartan was advised by two priests, Father Coyle and Father Daly, that this was not an IRB rising, but a rising inspired by Connolly. They did not want to take part it upon orders from Dublin. The arguing between Denis McCullough, the priests and McCartan went on all day. The priests maintained they would not leave their own parish and would advise their men against going off to join Liam Mellows. Later, they got news of a demobilisation order from Dublin.

McCullough decided that if the Tyrone men did not join him, there was no point in going to Galway and he returned to Belfast where the men were demobilised and told to go home. McCullough and most of his men were arrested and jailed the following week.

An article in the *Belfast Newsletter* of April 24th, 1916 seems to refer to events in Coalisland. It states:

> The districts of Dungannon and Coalisland were the centres of intense excitement in consequence of the visit of large parties of Sinn Féiners, a number of whom bore arms, from Dublin, Belfast and other places [...] Altogether one hundred and forty men were present, the majority of whom bore arms. A private conference took place in Coalisland at noon, but at 1.15pm, a motorist arrived from Dublin, and the news they brought seemed to have a disturbing effect, for the conference immediately broke up [...] on receipt of the news brought by the motorist, the Belfast and Dublin contingents were paraded and hurriedly marched to Cookstown. They left for home by the evening train.

Nora Connolly, Eilis Ní Chorra and four other members of the Belfast Cumann na mBan decided to go on to Dublin to let the Military Council know about the confusion. Arriving there on Easter Sunday morning, the news was brought to Connolly and preparations got underway to try to counter the confusion. A special meeting of the Military Council was convened and it was decided to proceed with the Rising on Easter Monday.

After being shown the Proclamation to memorise as best they could, the young women were sent north to inform activists that the Rising was to begin and they should proceed as planned.

Other Cumann na mBan members were sent to different parts of Ireland with orders for the Volunteers to proceed. Despite their best efforts, confusion reigned. The Sunday Independent carried a countermanding order from MacNéill, the head of the Irish Volunteers. Some newspapers also carried it on Easter Monday. Nora was sent back to Belfast by her father with the message that the Rising had started. She received a negative response from Denis McCullough who accepted MacNéill's countermanding order. She and her comrades then travelled back to Tyrone. Again MacNéill's order held. Eventually, in exasperation, the young women headed back to Dublin. The Rising at least had started there.

7. The Rising

Who fears to speak of Easter week?
Who dares their fate deplore?

The Irish Republic was proclaimed in Dublin on Easter Monday, April 24, at noon. The Proclamation was addressed to Irish men and women. It was a democratic document of, as of yet, unfulfilled social, political and economic intent. It pledged 'the right to religious and civil liberty equal right and opportunities' for all.

It promised to pursue the happiness of the whole nation and all its parts, cherishing all the children of the nation equally. It was anti-sectarian. It contained a commitment to national freedom and sovereignty and it affirmed the right of the people of Ireland to the ownership of Ireland.

The Proclamation was read by Patrick Pearse outside the GPO after the contingent of Irish Volunteers and Citizen Army had been ordered by Connolly to occupy the post office. Tom Clarke stood by Pearse's side. The garrison had marched to the GPO from Liberty Hall. Clarke, because of his age, went on ahead with Seán MacDiarmada who, limping, carried a stick. Before leaving Liberty Hall, Connolly addressed the assembled Irish Volunteers and Citizen Army. He said how pleased he was to see so many of them there because he had told the Citizen Army that if anyone did not want to fight, they could leave and nobody would have any recriminations against them or think little of them. Each man must do what he felt was right. Just as they left for the Rising, he said:

> Now when we start marching, each of you to the different posts you are going to, your first step you take after Pearse and Plunkett and myself, you form the Irish Republican Army.

In a statement issued the following day by Patrick Pearse announcing the Proclamation, he said:

> Simultaneously with the issue of the proclamation of the Provisional Government the Dublin division of the Army of the Republic, including the Irish Volunteers, Citizen Army;

> Hibernian Rifles, and other bodies, occupied dominating points in the city. The GPO was seized at 12 noon, the Castle was attacked at the same moment, and shortly afterwards the Four Courts were occupied. The Irish troops hold the City Hall and dominate the Castle. Attacks were immediately commenced by the British forces, and were everywhere repulsed. At the moment of writing this report (9.30am Tuesday) the republican forces hold all their positions and the British forces have nowhere broken through. There has been heavy and continuous fighting for nearly forty-eight hours, the casualties of the enemy being much more numerous than those on the republican side. The republican forces everywhere are fighting with splendid gallantry. The populace of Dublin are plainly with the Republic, and the officers and men are everywhere cheered as they march through the street. The whole centre of the city is in the hands of the Republic, whose flag flies from the GPO.
>
> Commandant General PH Pearse is Commander in Chief of the Army of the Republic and is President of the Provisional Government. Commandant General James Connolly is commanding the Dublin districts.
>
> Communication with the country is largely cut, but reports to hand show that the country is rising, and bodies of men from Kildare and Fingal have already reported in Dublin.

On the day that Pearse read the Proclamation, the British Lord Lieutenant Wimborne was to pay an informal visit to Belfast. He had expressed the wish to meet leading businessmen there. Lord Wimbourne had supported the Home Rule Bill in the Parliament.

The president of the Belfast Chamber of Commerce, Mr JH Stirling, had responded by writing a letter to the city's Lord Mayor.

> The Belfast commercial community in the north of Ireland does not want to meet Lord Wimborne because although the great questions are of equal interest to the business men of Belfast as to those of Manchester, the Home Rule question is of still greater importance. We cannot usefully discuss plans for 'commercial development after the war' until we know what form of government we shall have to work them out. The fiscal legislation of a Home Rule parliament might upset the best of them.

Meanwhile, back in Dublin, a 'Stop Press' edition of *Irish War News*, Vol 1, No 1, Tuesday, April 25th 1916 – it was the only edition issued – announced the declaration of the Irish Republic and the appointment of the Provisional Government. Belfast remained quiet.

The Easter holiday was spoiled by dismal weather. A torrential downpour of rain disrupted the day's soccer matches throughout the city and the sports meeting of pony and dog racing at Celtic Park. Heavy showers fell intermittently during the remainder of the day. The Proclamation of the Republic failed to reach the general populace of the city. Distillery beat Glenavon 2-0 while at Grosvenor Park, Linfield beat Belfast United 3-1. In Dublin, two British 18-pounder guns bombarded the city centre.

On Easter Tuesday, the *Belfast Newsletter* and the *Irish News* carried first reports of the Rising. The Newsletter reported the arrest of Roger Casement on April 21st, trying to smuggle German weapons into Ireland. It linked this event with the first news about 'disturbances' in Dublin on Easter Monday. The editorial declared:

> 'Every loyal subject of the King will rejoice at the fact that Sir Roger Casement has fallen into the hands of the British authorities and that he has been taken red-handed in an enterprise which could only have one object, the stirring up of a rebellion in Ireland.' It goes on to point out that they had always said that the nationalists could not be trusted and that 'the connection between the disloyalty movement in our country and Germany is now completed.'

It also mentioned that the British Viceroy Lord Wimborne did not turn up in Belfast.

It was business as usual for the UVF. All Belfast Volunteer Force members, able to do a day's duty, were to report at St George's market at 9am. The *Irish News* editorial called upon readers to:

> [...] 'keep cool' [...] It is certain that evil has been done – irrepairable evil from the personal point of view to many unhappy families, but not irrepairable from the nationalist standpoint. If the people of this country hold firmly to their principles, cleave to their leaders who brought them to the verge of victory – who sought to have the humblest and the most credulous of them from the consequences of

> suicidal folly – and keep their hearts sound and their heads cool in the face of dangers whom magnitude cannot be estimated at the present moment. KEEP COOL – DON'T GIVE WAY TO PANIC OR PASSION.'

Thousands of British reinforcements poured into Dubin.

As the fighting in Dublin moved into its third day and the British intensified their bombardment of Dublin by deploying the Admiralty gunboat Helga on the Liffey, Joe Devlin announced to a warm and sunny Belfast that he would preside at the final meeting of workers in connection with the flag day in aid of the Comfort Fund for the Belfast soldiers of the 16th Division. This would be held in the lecture hall of the Nationalist Club, Berry Street.

The unionists were obviously getting some accurate information from Dublin, at least enough to warrant an urgent meeting of regimental battalion commanders of the Ulster Volunteer Force. This meeting was held in the Old Town Hall 'with the objective of considering what steps should be taken to ensure the preservation of the peace and to prevent any action on the part of individuals which might occasion disorder'.

The *Newsletter* assured citizens that all was well. 'Members of the Belfast Volunteer Force were on duty during the day'.

The *Northern Whig* editorial was equally reassuring.

> We are confident that all classes in Ulster will, now that the holidays have ended, return to business as usual and that the good temper and the good feeling will continue. The authorities can be safely left to deal with the foolish and unpatriotic people who wish to disturb the peace of the nation. There is no part of the Empire where the imperialistic spirit is stronger than in Ulster.

The following day, martial law was proclaimed in Ireland and large reinforcements, ten thousand troops, arrived. Railway traffic to Dublin had been suspended from Tuesday and telephone and other communications with Dublin and the rest of the country were also broken off.

The *Northern Whig* was nonplussed. 'As far as Belfast is concerned, the city is in normal condition, no excitement, no apparent interferences with the ordinary course of business.'

Carson joined Redmond in saying that 'everything should be done to denounce and put down the rebels now and forever more'. Redmond, speaking on behalf of the Nationalist Party the 'overwhelming majority of the people of Ireland', spoke of feelings of 'detestation and horror' over what the rebels had done in Dublin.

British Prime Minister Asquith announced that:

> General Sir John Maxwell will leave this afternoon and has been given plenary powers under Martial Law, the Irish executive has placed themselves under his disposal. His authority is absolute.

No party in the British Parliament made any objections. Back in Belfast the Volunteer Defence Force appealed for recruits.

> A thousand men are urgently needed for service in the Belfast Volunteer Defence Corps. Applications can be made at the Headquarters, 14a High Street, Belfast.

On Friday Connolly was wounded. The British artillery was now using incendiary shells. The IRA leadership decided to evacuate the women from the GPO. Winifred Carney refused to leave.

The day before in a manifesto Connolly said:

> I am satisfied that we should have accomplished more [...] had our arrangements for a simultaneous rising of the whole country with a combined plan as sound as the Dublin plan been allowed.

Then magnanimously he ended: 'Both Eoin MacNéilI and we have acted in the best interests of Ireland'.

On Saturday, April 29th 1916, Pearse announced an unconditional surrender. Against all the odds the republican forces had held out for a week against the might of the British empire. During the fighting between one hundred and sixty and two hundred and sixteen civilians were killed and injured. Of the twenty thousand British troops involved, five hundred and sixteen officers and men were officially listed as killed, wounded or missing. Sixty-four republicans were killed in action during the Rising. It was a bloody first week for the Irish Republic. The IRA, Cumann na mBan and Fianna numbered no more than about one thousand five hundred. They were armed only with shoulder weapons and hand guns.

8. We shall rise again

'Damn your concessions England, we want our country.'

Seán MacDiarmada

In the aftermath of the rising there were one hundred and sixty courts martial and one hundred twenty-two sentenced- ninety-seven death sentences were commuted to penal servitude. Several thousand men and women were deported to various British prison and internment camps. Fourteen of the leaders and Tom Kent from Cork were executed by firing squad. Roger Casement was later hanged in England.

The *Irish Catholic* described the rising as insane and criminal and Cardinal Logue telegraphed the Pope: 'insurrection happily terminated'. The Freeman's Journal reported how the Vatican 'greatly praised' the Irish clergy for the zeal with which they had supported the British efforts to restore order.

In Belfast the *Irish News* declared:

> The rebels of old fought for Ireland because they had no other alternative and because the evils of the situation demanded desperate remedies.

The following day, May 3rd , the British executed Tom Clarke, Patrick Pearse and Thomas MacDonagh. The *Irish Catholic* described Pearse as a 'crazy and insolent Schoolteacher' and his comrades as 'rogues and fools'. The Catholic Bishop of Limerick took the opposite view and condemned the executions. The British House of Commons, including Redmondites applauded at the announcement of the first executions. One nationalist MP screamed 'murder' at his fellow members. George Bernard Shaw was the first public figure in England to protest at British policy.

The *Irish News* was not impressed:

> There was not a 'national uprising' in Dublin. It was not even a sectional 'uprising'. The whole sad business was conceived, planned and carried into fatal effect without the knowledge or the sanction of the Irish Nation.

On May 4th four other leaders were shot. They were Joseph Plunkett, Edward Daly, Michael O'Hanrahan and Willie Pearse. Plunkett married Grace Gifford in the chapel in Kilmainham a few hours before he was shot. The next day John MacBride was executed.

The *Irish News* hesitated:

> Eight leaders have now been shot. We hold that an end should be made to the Dublin executions at this stage. The leaders have paid the fullest penalty. Ireland never had other feelings that horror for their actions, but there has been more than enough of bloodshed.

Ceannt, Mallin, Heuston and Colbert were shot dead on the 8th, Thomas Kent of Cork on the 9th. It was rumoured that there would be ninety executions. Redmond was moved to ask that the executions be halted.

The *Irish News* echoed his call:

> Not merely 'large sections' as Redmond says, but all sections of the Irish people now regard the continued gratification of this blood-lust with bitterness, exasperation and horror.

Slowly the Irish establishment was being forced to change its stance as news of the executions swept the country. The British by their brutality were alienating their allies in Ireland. From condemnation came a retreat to grudging admiration and near applause as they tried to catch up on nationalist opinion which was to swinging behind the republicans.

In Belfast the *Irish News* lead the retreat:

> Twelve men in Dublin have suffered the death penalty by order of Courtmartial [...] Hundreds of innocent people are arrested, hundreds are deported. There has been more gross' injustice wreaked on inoffensive people throughout Ireland during the past week than within the past fifty years. Not only the executions, but the behaviour of British forces throughout the country, house searches, arrests etc, cause anger among the Irish people. Searches and arrests were taking place in districts which had remained quiet.

In Dublin the *Independent* reminded the world that Connolly was still alive, seriously wounded and a prisoner in Dublin Castle. Its editorial called for his execution: 'Let the worst of the ringleaders be singled out and dealt with as they deserve.'

The Belfast unionist press said little about the executions. The *Northern Whig* ridiculed Redmond's plea for an end to the executions: 'Redmonites have for some days shown symptoms of desperate uneasiness in view of the executions of the rebels' [...] due to 'a fear of losing support among the Irish people'.

It is also reported at this time that the Archbishop of Armagh had written to the Times asking for a merciful treatment of the rebels by allowing the less guilty ones to opt for serving with the British Army on the Continent. The *Belfast Telegraph* harboured no such illusions:

> Every man knew perfectly well the consequences involved in the failure of their scheme. If the Government wishes to discourage all further attempts of the kind, the one way to do so is to make clear now that there will be no trifling with treason. Mercy to traitors is rank injustice to the loyal.

Later on May 10th:

> Sir John Maxwell's rule has been a blessing to Ireland and we trust that the efforts which are being made to interfere with his discretion will prove a failure.

By now, of those who signed the Proclamation, only Connolly and MacDiarmada remained.

In New York, the following day, the Evening Post's Washington correspondent reported that many sympathisers with the English were pained and alienated because they believed that the reprisals against the Irish rebels were carried too far. A resolution expressing the horror of the American people at the executions in Ireland, was introduced in the House of Representatives by Mr Dwyer from Missouri. It was referred to the Foreign Affairs Committee, which declared that 'no action will be taken by the US Government because the question involves the internal affairs of a foreign Government'.

At dawn that same morning Seán MacDiarmada, crippled with arthritis and unable to walk, was executed in Kilmainham.

Later they carried Connolly on a stretcher and propped him up in a chair. He gripped the sides of the chair to steady himself and held his head high waiting for the volley.

Lillie, his wife and daughter Nora had been brought to see him late the night before. He told them he was to be shot at dawn.

Lillie was crying, her head on his bed, weeping heartbreakingly.

'Don't cry Lillie,' he pleaded. 'You'll unman me.'

'But your beautiful life, James,' she sobbed. 'Your beautiful life.'

'Hasn't it been a full life Lillie,' he said 'and isn't this a good end?'

Nora was crying too. He surreptitiously slipped her his last statement made at his court martial.

> Believing that the British government has no right in Ireland, never had any right in Ireland, and never can have any right in Ireland, the presence, in any generation of Irishmen, of even a respectable minority, ready to die to affirm that truth, make that government for ever a usurpation and a crime against human progress.

He talked quietly to Lillie, trying to make little jokes.

'The papers say that the British government promised that there would be no more executions,' Nora sobbed.

'England's promises,' her father smiled at her.

Lillie collapsed, and was revived. James tried to hold her but could not. 'Time Up' said the guard.

Nora laid her hand on his.

'Good-bye,' he said 'go to your mother'.

Nora could not move Lillie. Eventually a nurse put her arms around her and took her away.

Nora ran back to her father and kissed him. He held her close.

'I'm proud of you,' he said.

He looked across to where Lillie stood in the cell door way.

'We shall rise again,' he whispered.

Kilmainham Prison
Dublin
May 11th 1916.

My Dear Daly

Just a wee note to bid you Good Bye. I expect in a few hours to join Tom and the other heroes in a better world. I have been sentenced to a soldier's death – to be shot tomorrow morning. I have nothing to say about this only that I look on it as a part of the day's work. We die that the Irish nation may live. Our blood will re-baptise and reinvigorate the old land. Knowing this it is superfluous to say how happy I feel. I know now what I have always felt, that the Irish nation can never die. Let present day place hunters condemn our action as they will, posterity will judge us aright from the effects of our action.

I know I will meet you soon, until then Good Bye. God guard and protect you and all in No 15. You have had a sore trial, but I know quite well that Mrs Daly and all the girls feel proud in spite of a little temporary and natural grief, that her son, & the girls, their brother as well as Tom are included in the list of honours. Kindly remember me specially to Mrs Clarke and tell her I am the same Seán that she always knew.

God Bless you all
As ever
Sincerely yours
Seán Mac Diarmada

Letter from Seán Mac Diarmada written from Kilmainham prison

Drawings of Frongoch internment camp

Postscript

The following extract from T.J. Campbell's *Fifty Years of Ulster* is a sympathetic account of a meeting in Belfast in the aftermath of the Easter Rising. It provides an interesting postscript to our story.

The St Mary's Hall Conference 1916

A piquant situation arose in the North. Redmond received what he thought was the firm offer, through Lloyd George from the government, to bring the Home Rule Act into immediate operation, subject to the temporary exclusion of the six Ulster counties, now known as Northern Ireland. The nationalist leaders agreed to this scheme. As the world knows, their hopes were dashed.

How would the Northern nationalists take the offer? Would they accept or reject temporary exclusion? A conference was held on June 23rd 1916, in St Mary's Hall. The proceedings were not open to the Press. I was not present, having been resident in Dublin from December 10th 1910, till February 16th 1922, though often in Belfast on professional work. What happened at the conference is known. Redmond, Dillon and Devlin attended and counselled the delegates to accept the temporary exclusion of the Six Counties as the best means of achieving the goal of a united self-governed nation on an early date. Redmond in emphatic words intimated that he would at once resign the leadership of the Party if his policy should fail to find endorsement. Dillon and Devlin stood by Redmond. The threat of resignation carried immense, almost coercive, weight. Devlin's prestige thrown on Redmond's side was decisive. By a huge majority the compromise was ratified. It was an agonising decision, entailing an assent to the secession of the Six Counties from Ireland though only for a short spell and to the retention of the Six Counties during that short spell under British rule.

The following official report of the proceedings was issued that night:

> A Conference of the representative nationalists of the Six Counties principally affected by the proposals of Mr Lloyd George in connection with the Government of Ireland was held today in St Mary's Hall, Belfast, at 12 o'clock noon. The following was the basis of representation:
>
> 1. One priest in each parish in the Six Counties;
> 2. Nationalist members of Parliament in the Six Counties;
> 3. The officers of the Divisional Executives of the UIL for each constituency in the Six Counties;
> 4. The County officers of the Ancient Order of Hibernians, the District officers of the Irish National Foresters in the Six Counties;
> 5. All National members of elected public boards in the Six Counties;
> 6. For the cities of Belfast and Derry five additional members elected by the Executives of the UIL, INF and AOH.
>
> The number of delegates entitled to attend was 1,077; the number actually present was 776. Mr John E Redmond, MP, Chairman of the Irish Parliamentary Party, presided. The chairman having addressed the Conference, Mr Patrick Dempsey; JP, TC, Belfast, proposed the following resolution:
>
> That this Conference of representatives from the Counties of Antrim, Down, Derry, Armagh, Tyrone and Fermanagh, and from the Cities of Belfast and Derry, having considered proposals of Mr Lloyd George for the temporary and provisional settlement of the Irish difficulty, is of opinion that they should be accepted, and that in view of all the circumstances of the present situation in Ireland they offer the best means of carrying on the fight for a united and self-governing Ireland.
>
> The resolution was seconded by the Very Rev Canon McCarton, PP, Donaghmore, County Tyrone. The resolution was supported by the Very Rev Canon Quinn, Pp, VG, Camlough, County Armagh, National Director

> UIL, the Very Rev John Nolan, Pp, VF, Moneyglass, Toomebridge, Co Antrim: Mr John Dillon, MP, and Mr Joseph Devlin, MP. The resolution was opposed by Mr F J O'Connor, solicitor, Omagh; Mr T McLoughlin, UDC, Armagh; the Very Rev W B MacFeely; PP, BD, Glendermot, Waterside, Derry; the Very Rev Canon Keown, PP, VG, Enniskillen; Mr John McGlone, National Director, UIL Mid-Armagh, and Alderman James McCarron, Derry.
>
> No amendment was moved to the resolution, and at the close of the discussion a division was taken by open vote, the name of every delegate rising in his place and declaring his vote, 'Yes' or 'No'. Messrs Daniel McCann, Belfast, and T J S Harbinson, solicitor; were appointed scrutineers, and after the counting of the votes announced the result as follows: For the resolution 475, against 265; majority for the resolution 210. The proceedings, which were characterised by great earnestness and entire good feeling throughout, then concluded.

Next day, the National Directory of the United Irish league accepted the settlement. A vital difference of opinion immediately afterwards was manifested. The Ulster Unionist Council maintained that the exclusion of the Six Counties was intended to be final and definite. The nationalists maintained that the exclusion was but a temporary expedient or the duration of the war, and that the whole position would be open to revision in a conference that would follow the conclusion of the war.

On the evening of the St Mary's Hall Conference, Lord Selborne (unionist), President of the Board of Agriculture, resigned office in protest against the proposed settlement. On June 25th, Asquith announced that the unionist members of the cabinet had refused to agree to one of the principal terms of the settlement which provided for the continuance of the Irish members in the Imperial Parliament at their full strength. Redmond refused to agree to the variation, which he stigmatised as a disgraceful breach of faith.

Lord Landsdowne and Walter long declared they would never agree to the terms Redmond had submitted to his people in Lloyd George's name. It looked as if the Cabinet was not going to be bound by the compromise. On July l0th in the House of Commons, Asquith, answering Carson, announced that the Six Counties could only be brought under an Irish Government by a special Act, and only with their own consent. He explained that the settlement was a provisional measure.

The 12th of July that year was marked in Belfast by five minutes of silence as the thousands of Irish dead from the slaughter of the Battle of the Somme were mourned. On July 13th Lord Lansdowne, a member of the government, stated that the settlement would be permanent as regards the exclusion of part of Ulster.

Three weeks later, on August 3rd, Roger Casement was hanged in Pentonville Prison, London.

Appendix

The following is a statement from Denis McCullough, then living in Ranelagh, Dublin in 1942 in relation to a pension application from the Free State government for his service with the Irish Volunteers in the North around 1916. The document is in the Archives Department, University College Dublin and was supplied by Raymond Quinn.

On my release from Belfast Prison in November 1915, where I had received a six-months' sentence under D.O.R.A. for refusal to leave Ireland under a Military Order to do so, it was decided by the H.Q. to appoint a man to take military charge in Ulster. Mr. Burke (now Dr. Burke, U.C.D.) was appointed and I was summoned to Dublin to meet him and receive orders for future activities. The meeting was arranged in the Keating Branch premises; there were present Commandants Pearse and Connolly, Mr. Burke and myself. Instructions were given to Mr. Burke and to myself. Mine were, that on receipt of a coded message indicating the date of the Rising, I was to proceed to Tyrone, with as many men as possible, make contact with the leaders there, and proceed with them, with all possible speed to Connaught, where we were to join Mellowes [sic] and act with him on any orders he had received. I pointed out that we were very badly armed, having only about 40 rifles amongst us, of mixed calibre, from Howth Guns and Snyders, to small Martini-Enfields, with about ten rounds for each. I suggested that both to secure our rear and get additional arms and ammunition, we would have to attack and take any Police Barracks we met en route. Commandant Connolly, endorsed by Commandant Pearse, immediately jumped on this suggestion and said it must not be attempted in any circumstances. He finally said, 'You will fire no shot in Ulster. You will leave it with all possible speed, join Mellows in Connaught and do the best you can there'. He further said, 'If we win through, we can think of Ulster and deal with it then. You will accept this as an order and obey it'. Pearse subsequently gave me the coded message I was to receive. I understood that Mr. Burke was to convey these orders to the leaders in Tyrone and elsewhere in Ulster. He was provided with a new Sunbeam Motor-Cycle to enable him to carry out his duties, over the Province. I returned to Belfast and made my plans in accordance with these instructions.

In the meantime, Alf Cotton (now, I think in the Department of Defence) had been ordered by the Military Authorities to leave Kerry and reside in Belfast. He was instructed by Commandant-General Pearse to obey this order and to report to me every day, in case I received any orders for him. On the Saturday preceding Easter Saturday 1916 he called and informed me that he had received a despatch from Pearse, ordering him to Kerry with arms and equipment and enclosing £10 to pay his expenses.

He was to be there 'by hook or by crook' on Easter Saturday. I immediately interpreted this as meaning that action was to start on Easter Saturday or Sunday. I, personally, received no orders, nor did the promised code arrive. I started from Dublin immediately, saw Seán McDermott on Monday and learned from him that the Rising would start on Easter Sunday. I returned to Belfast, mobilized my men and gave them instructions to travel to Tyrone on Easter Saturday, for week-end manoeuvres, providing the necessary money for their additional equipment and for train fares. I told none of them the real purpose of the manoeuvres, thinking it safer to keep this to myself. Some of the section leaders guessed however, I believe, and all turned out as ordered.

On the Good Friday, a Mr. Hackett of Clogher, Co. Tyrone, arrived at my place with a car and a request from some of the

Tyrone leaders to meet them that evening at Dr. McCartan's house at Carrickmore.

Having all my local arrangements completed, I travelled down to Carrickmore with Mr. Hackett. I there met Mr. Burke, O.C. Ulster, Dr. Pat. McCartan, Father Daly and Father Coyle. Long discussions took place, during which the priests declared that the proposed Rising was purely an attempt by Connolly and his Party to rush the Volunteers into premature action. They were convinced that Professor MacNeill and the Volunteer Executive were not behind it. I detailed my interview with Seán McDermott and Tom Clarke and informed them that I was satisfied that a full authenticated Rising was coming off; that I was bringing my men down from Belfast to take part in it and urged them to make the necessary preparations to co-operate with me and carry out the orders I had received. They were of opinion that these orders were stupid and suicidal and impossible to carry out, taking no account of the ground we had to cover, mostly through hostile Orange territory, before we reached even the Connaught Border. They had doubt about the good faith behind the whole proposals. I eventually invited them to send to Dublin and satisfy themselves on the matter in doubt. It was then agreed that Dr. McCartan, who did not share the opinions expressed by the clergymen, should go to Dublin and bring back the exact facts of the situation, as he found them there. At all events, Mr. Burke, O.C. Ulster, did not appear again and dropped out of the picture.

On Easter Saturday morning, I got Hugh Rodgers of Beragh, to go to Belfast in his Ford Car, contact Peter Burns there, who, meantime had got our guns and ammunition removed outside the City; load these and bring them to an old disused schoolhouse or hall I had procured near Coalisland. Rodgers arrived safely at Coalisland the same evening; we got the arms etc. safely depôted as arranged. I got out my own automatic, and on the way back to Dr. McCartan's house, after leaving Hugh Rodgers' car, I was examining it, when on pulling the trigger there was a shell in the chamber and the bullet went through my left hand. I got to Dr. McCartan's house where the wound was dressed, and I was put to bed until Dr. McCartan arrived back from Dublin, later in the evening. The two priests had returned and Dr. McCartan put his report before them. They were still opposed to the proposed action, and no decision was arrived at, after a long and somewhat acrimonious discussion. For some reason, which I cannot now remember, it was decided to send further messengers to Dublin for further information, and Miss McCartan and Miss Owens of Beragh were sent. A further meeting was to be held at midnight, when word was received from them.

In the meantime, I had learned that the first contingent of my men had arrived at Coalisland; that a second contingent was to follow, and a few to complete the number would come on Sunday morning.

No mobilization had taken place or had been arranged for, in Tyrone, pending the final conference, which took place around the midnight of Easter Saturday night. The whole ground was covered again and again.

The Tyrone leaders finally decided that they would not leave their own districts but would take action there. I could not agree to this and in the end stated that unless they were prepared to join me and carry out the orders they had received, I would bring my men back to Belfast in the morning. This, not being acceptable, the Conference broke up and I determined to act as I had stated. Accordingly, after a few hours sleep, Dr. McCartan drove me to Coalisland. I gathered the men under their section leaders, explained the position briefly to them, and ordered them back to Belfast. There was some grumbling, but all carried out orders and started across Tyrone for Cookstown to entrain for Belfast. I, personally, decided to make for Dublin and take my chance in the fighting there. I induced Dr. McCartan to drive me to intercept the train to Dublin at Portadown, but the steering gear of his car broke down and it ran into a ditch not far from

Coalisland. I procured a sidecar and proceeded after the men and accompanied them to Cookstown, via Stewartstown, where we were attacked by an Orange crowd some revolver shots being fired and one of our men arrested. A rescue attempt was being organised, but I succeeded in preventing it. We reached Belfast safely and the men dispersed. All the arms and ammunition was safely depôted in Tyrone.

I was arrested about ten days later, with a number of the other prominent Belfast Volunteers, brought to Richmond Barracks, Dublin, and eventually to Knutsford Prison. After a few days there, I was taken out and put in solitary confinement, in a separate wing of the prison, where I was later joined by a few others. I remained there until I was removed to Frongoch, under separate guard and put in the North Camp by myself, under special guard until Terence McSwiney and Thomas McCurtin arrived, when they were put in with me. We were removed to the South Camp where all the other prisoners were, after a few days. I was immediately elected Vice-Commandant of the Camp, under Col. Ginger O'Connell and retained this position until I was removed with the other Camp Leaders to Reading Gaol, where I remained until my release early in August 1916.

From the preceding details, it will be seen that I carried out the orders I had received from Comdt. Gen. Padraig Pearse, though I received no direct orders for the actual Rising. The men under my command also turned out. It was not their fault that they took no part in the fighting. They acted under my orders and I acted on my own responsibility in sending them back to Belfast. Neither was it my fault that the orders I received were not completed. I was ordered to 'join the Tyrone men and proceed to Connaught'. If the Tyrone men would not come, it would be fruitless for me to attempt such a journey with my handful of half- armed men, but we were on the spot to do as ordered. I am not blaming the Tyrone leaders, who, I believe, acted correctly, but that does not alter the facts I set out.

I was in prison from April to August 1916, and suggest that this should count as Military Service under the Act, both for myself and for the men with me, about whose cases I am concerned.

I set out the foregoing facts for two purposes. First, in support of my claim and those of my colleagues of the period, from Belfast. The fact that we were able to mobilize in Tyrone, with all the arms and ammunition we had ready for action, was a noteworthy feat, as only the people in Belfast know the conditions under which we acted. Secondly, I want to put these facts, as I see and remember them now, on record for historical purposes, in case anyone ever wishes to know what happened in the North in 1916.

Frongoch Internees

In the wake of 1916, many republicans were shipped to English jails and from there brought to Frongoch Internment Camp in north Wales. There are 24 listed as coming from Belfast.

Jerry Barnes, 66 St James Park
Frank Bootie, Alexander Street West
Peter Burns, 7 Linden Street
Mick Carolan, 80 Chief Street
Thomas Clear, 57 Agincourt Avenue
Alex Connolly, 2 Alamanda Terrace, Falls Road
Joseph Connolly, 38 Divis Street
Alfie Cotton, 2 Rosemount Gardens
Patrick Dempsey, 40 Locan Street, Broadway
Henry Dobbyn, 21 Clonard Gardens
Seamus Dobbyn, 21 Clonard Gardens
Robert Haskin, c/o Coolfin Street, Donegall Road
Sam Herron, Doris Street
James Johnston, Shandown Road, Knock
John Kelly, Iris Street
Denis McCullough, Grosvenor Road
Charles McDowell, 19 Locan Street
Pat Nash, 52 Gibson Street
Sean Neeson, 153 Falls Road
Harry Osborne, 69 Smithfield
Cathal Shannon, 27 Canning Street
James Smith, 3 Somerville Gardens, Andersonstown
Edward Tierney, Falls Road
Thomas Wilson, 248 Albert Bridge Road

Biographical Notes

ALICE MILLIGAN, was born in 1865 in Omagh, County Tyrone, as daughter of Seaton F. Milligan, a wealthy businessman and antiquary. She was educated at the Methodist College, Belfast, Magee College in Derry and King's College in London. She refused to go to Germany to learn the language and instead went to Dublin to learn Irish. Her studies intensified her enthusiasm for the political independence of Ireland. Together with Ethna Carbery, she edited a national literary magazine Shan Van Vocht (Poor Old Woman) based in Belfast in 1896. It included the early writings of Connolly, but the editors made it clear they disagreed with his socialism.

She was organiser for the Gaelic league for some years and toured the country producing historical tableaux to raise funds to finance Irish classes and was supported in that by WB Yeats and George Russell. She died at Tyrcar, Omagh, on May 13th 1953.

ETHNA CARBERY (pseudonym for ANNA JOHNSON) was born in 1866 in Ballymena, County Antrim. She edited Shan Van Vocht together with Alice Milligan (the magazine folded in 1899). She attended the inaugural meeting of Inghinidhe na hEireann (Daughters of Erin) in October 1900 and was involved in its activities. Her publications include poetry, the Four Winds of Eirinn and collected short stories as the Passionate Hearts and In the Celtic past. She married the writer Seamus MacManus.

On April 14th 1916, Connolly asked her to come to Dublin. She helped with preparations for the Rising, typing dispatches and mobilisation orders in Liberty Hall in Dublin. As a member of Cumann na mBan and the Irish Citizen Army, she was one of the last to leave the GPO. She had refused to leave the wounded Connolly. After the Rising she was interned, first in Mountjoy Prison, later in Aylesbery Prison together with Helena Molony and Countess Markievicz. She was released in December 1916.

Like most of the women in Cumann na mBan, she rejected the Treaty and was wary of the Free State governments, including de Valera's. She did not feel this was the state she had fought for.

WINIFRED CARNEY, born at Fishershill, Bangor, on December 4th 1887, was reared in Belfast, living at 5 Falls Road. She always lived with and cared for her mother and nursed her in her old age. She married George McBride in September 1928. Winnie was educated at the Christian Brother school in Donegall Street in Belfast. There she worked for a short period as a junior teacher, later she qualified as one of the first ladies secretaries and short-hand typists at Hughs Commercial Academy. She worked for a short time as a clerk in a solicitor's office in Dungannon. She was very interested in literature and art and was a good singer and piano player. She had a keen interest in the Gaelic revival and Irish history and learned Irish.

In her early twenties she became involved in suffragette and socialist activities in Belfast. Winifred was a good friend of Mary Johnston, married to the leader of the Irish labour Party, Thomas Johnston. The couple were good friends with James Connolly. When Mary fell ill, she asked Winnie to take over her job as union secretary. Winnie was then 24 years old, and moved to the little union office at 50 York Street.

THOMAS CLARKE was born on the Isle of Wight, England, of Irish parents, in 1858. He spent his early childhood in South Africa but returned from there to Dungannon, County Tyrone, when he was ten. As a young man he went to America where he joined, Clan na Gael, an Irish American organisation which was closely associated with the Fenians. He was captured in England on a Fenian mission in 1883 and spent 16 years in English convict jails. At the age of 35 he was able to write from prison that he had spent almost a third of his life in jail.

On his release, broken in health, but not in spirit, he set about re-organising the IRB and planning a rising against the English. He fought in the GPO in Easter Week. A Fenian to the end, he was shot in Kilmainham on May 3rd 1916.

PADRAIG PEARSE, described as 'the greatest of the great men of Easter Week', was born in Dublin, 1879. He was educated by the Christian Brothers and became a barrister. He learned to speak Irish as well as he spoke English, he also wrote prose, poetry and plays in both languages. He founded Scoil Eanna, a school for boys, and many of his pupils fought beside him in Easter Week. An orator of extraordinary power, his oration over the grave of O'Donovon Rossa in 1915 will never be forgotten: 'Ireland unfree shall never be at peace'.

A member of the Military Council of the IRB, he was Commander in Chief of the Provisional Government. To the court martial which tried him after the surrender, he said: 'When I was a child of ten, I went on my bare knees to my bedside one night and promised God that J should devote my life to an effort to free my country. J have kept my promise.' He was shot in Kilmainham on May 3rd 1916.

SEÁN MacDIARMADA was born in Kiltyclogher, County Leitrim, in 1883. Through the influence of Thomas Clarke and through his association with the Gaelic League, he came to devote himself to the cause of Irish freedom, and, as national organiser of the IRB, he travelled Ireland enlisting members. He contracted a severe illness which left him with a limp.

He took an active part in the formation of the Irish Volunteers, and organised units of the IRB all over the country. He was a member of the Military Council which planned the Rising of Easter Week and, despite lameness and ill-health, took his place besides his comrades in the GPO. He was shot in Kilmainham on May 12th 1916.

JAMES CONNOLLY was born in 1868. His parents emigrated to Edinburgh. He started to work there when he was only a child of eleven. He came to Ireland and later emigrated to America where he spent three years before coming back to Ireland to organise the labour movement. He helped to form the Irish Citizen Army, which joined with the Irish Volunteers at Easter 1916.

Commandant-general of the Dublin Division, Irish Republican Army, during Easter Week, he was badly wounded in the fighting in the General Post Office. When sentenced to death by the British, he was brought in an ambulance to Kilmainham on May 12th 1916, and shot. He was the last of the Easter Week men to be executed in Kilmainham.

ROGER CASEMENT was born in Co Dublin in 1864 and entered the British Civil Service in 1891. Casement gained worldwide admiration and praise for his exposure of the savage treatment meted out to the Congolese people slaving on the rubber plantations in their own country. He was knighted as a mark of respect for his good work which he continued with investigation into the barbaric treatment of the native South American people working on the rubber-plantations in the Amazon region.

Returning to Ireland in 1913, he threw himself into the cause of freedom at home and became a founder member of the Volunteers. After unsuccessfully trying to form an Irish Brigade from among the Irish prisoners of war in Germany, he travelled home to Ireland in a German U-boat carrying a consignment of weapons, but was arrested by the British when he arrived at Banna Strand, County Kerry, on Good Friday, 1916. Charged with 'treason' he was put on trial in London and condemned to death on June 29th. During the trial and the campaign for Casement's reprieve, the British government circulated forged copies of his diaries to undermine the campaign and try to make his execution acceptable.

Roger Casement was hanged in Pentonville Prison, London, on August 3rd 1916.

THOMAS MacDONAGH was born in Cloughjordan, County Tipperary, in 1873. He was educated at Rockwell College, Cashel. Poet, playwright and teacher, he became associated with Pearse in the Gaelic League, and was his friend and helper in the foundation of Scoil Eanna.

Director of Organisation in the Irish Volunteers, he was in command during Easter Week in Jacob's factory where his brother, Joseph, also fought. Believing that it should be a fight to the finish, he agreed to surrender only after much persuasion. He was shot in Kilmainham on May 3rd 1916.

JOSEPH MARY PLUNKETT, son of Count Plunkett, was born in Dublin in 1887. Though he was delicate from childhood, his ill health did not prevent him taking an active part in advancing the cause of Ireland. A close friend of Thomas MacDonagh, he too was a poet and enthusiast of the Irish language.

He was one of the founders of the Irish Volunteers in 1913 and later, as a member of the IRB, he travelled on secret missions to Germany and the USA. He was Director of Military Operations in the Volunteers and prepared the plans for the Rising of 1916. He left a sick bed to take part in the fighting in the General Post Office.

The youngest of the signatories of the Proclamation of the Irish Republic, he was married to Grace Gifford in the chapel in Kilmainham a few hours before he was shot there on May 4th 1916.

EAMONN CEANNT, son of an RIC man, was born in County Galway in 1881. His parents moved to Dublin while he was still a boy. He was educated by the Christian Brothers and joined the Gaelic League which was his introduction to republicanism. He was interested in traditional Irish music and other aspects of Irish culture. A member of the Irish Volunteers from the start, he was in command at the South Dublin Union in Easter Week. He was shot in Kilmainham on May 8th 1916.

EOIN MacNÉILL was born in Glenarm, County Antrim, and was educated at St Malachy's College, Belfast. He studied Old, Middle and Modern Irish at the University College in Dublin. He became vice-president of the Gaelic league on its foundation and later its President. He took the lead in the formation of the Irish National Volunteers in November 1913, and assumed editorship of the Irish Volunteer, the official paper of the organisation. As Easter 1916 drew near it was known that the

Volunteers were to hold Easter manoeuvres, which were to be taken part in by all branches in Ireland.

These were unexpectedly cancelled by a pronouncement signed by him. With this order MacNéill's association with the activities of the Volunteers ceased. Early in Easter Week he was arrested, and later tried by a general court-martial on charges of attempting to cause disaffection among the civil population and of inciting in a way likely to prejudice recruiting. He was sentenced to penal servitude for life, but was later released.

JAMES R (JACK) WHITE, was born in Broughshane, near Ballymena, as the son of Sir George White. Educated at Sandhurst, he commissioned in the Gordon Highlanders in 1897. He fought in the Boer War in South Africa, winning a DSO, and later served in India. On his return to Ireland he supported Home Rule. Soon he was completely involved with the nationalist cause. He became a member of the Gaelic league and supported Larkin during the lock-out of 1913. He trained the Irish Citizen Army and drilled the men at Croydon Park in Dublin. He was arrested during a workers' march to the Mansion House in 1914. Later, dissatisfied with the ICA he left it in May 1914 and became organiser in Derry and Tyrone for the Irish Volunteers. He was dismissed from their ranks when he called on Britain to recognise them as an Irish defence force.

Following the Easter Rising he organised a Welsh miners, strike to save James Connolly and was imprisoned at Pentonville Prison. He later settled in the north of Ireland and wrote an autobiography Misfits in 1930.

EDWARD CARSON, 1854-1935. Born in Dublin he became a barrister first in his home town and later in London. He was prosecuting counsel in the trial of Oscar Wilde. As an MP he represented Trinity College at Westminster from 1892 and he became leader of the Irish Unionists in 1910.

When Asquith's Home Rule Bill was introduced in 1912, he mobilised Protestant Ulster against it, playing a leading part in the formation of the UVF. He told the men not to be afraid of 'illegalities'. Carson was appointed Attorney-General in 1915 but resigned the same year in dissatisfaction with the conduct of the war. After the Easter Rising he was assured by Lloyd George that the Six Counties would be permanently excluded from the Home Rule Act of 1914 and he accepted office as First lord of the Admiralty.

When the war ended he became MP for the Duncairn division of Belfast. The Government of Ireland Act of 1920 was supported by the unionists on the advice of Carson as their only alternative since there was no hope of repealing the Home Rule Act. In 19211 he was appointed lord of Appeal and took a life peerage as Baron Carson of Duncairn

He died on October 22nd 1935, received a state funeral and is buried in St Anne's Cathedral.

References

Many thanks to the staff of the Belfast Central Library and to the Linenhall Library for their assistance and co-operation. Tá mé buioch daoibh. The sources of information for *Who Fears to Speak... ?* include:

Newspapers:

Irish News;
Belfast Telegraph;
Belfast Newsletter;
Northern Whig;
Irish Independent.

Weeklies:

Workers Republic;
Irish Freedom;
The Nation;
The National Volunteer;
The Irish Volunteer;
Eire;
Sunday Press;
Andersonstown News.

Books:

The Road to the Somme, by Phillip Orr, 1987.

The Irish Regiments in World War 1, by HED Harris.

Edward Carson, by ATQ Stewart.

Eoin MacNeill, Scholar and Man of Action, by Michael Tierney, 1980.

History of the Irish Citizen Army, by James Duffy, 1944.

Roger Casement, by Brian Inglis, 1973.

Casement, The Flawed Hero, by R. Sawyer, 1984.

The Lives of Roger Casement, by B.L. Reid, 1976.

Unmanageable Revolutionaries, by Margaret Ward, 1983.

Northern Ireland, the Orange State, by Michael Farrell, 1980.

The Protestants of Ulster, by Geoffrey Bell, 1987.

Ireland Her Own, by T.A. Jackson, 1985.

The Longest War, by Kevin Kelly, 1988.

James Connolly Selected Writings, Ed by P. Berresford Ellis, 1973.

Falls Memories, by Gerry Adams.

The Politics of Irish Freedom, by Gerry Adams.

Fifty Years Of Ulster, by T.J. Campbell.

The Irish Republic, by Dorothy MacArdle.

Portrait of a Rebel Father, by Nora Connolly O'Brien.

The Evolution of Sinn Fein, by R.M. Henry.

We Shall Rise Again, by Nora Connolly O'Brien.

A Dictionary of Irish Biography, Second Edition, by Henry Boylan.

A Dictionary of Irish History since 1800, by D.J. Hickey and J.E. Doherty.

The Divine Gospel Of Discontent, by Fergus O'Hare.

Liam Mellows and the Irish Revolution, by Desmond Greaves.

The Life and Times of James Connolly, by Desmond Greaves

Report of the Royal Commission on the Rebellion in Ireland, 1916.

The Capuchin Annual: 'A Rebel Remembers', by Eilis Ni Chorra.